A Time to Hope

In the wake of criminal behaviour by those most trusted, and floundering; and hopeless responses by the shepherds, where might the church find hope? Paul Castley acknowledges the anguish and loss that accompanies us, but reframes our experience through the ancient pairing of lament and hope. Expressing shame and grief in our prayer is healing and life giving, opening us to accept the Spirit's invitation to hope.

Jim Monaghan, Vicar General,
Catholic Diocese of Port Pirie.

While there are many reasons for Christians to grieve or lament today - such as their own failures in faithfulness, the failures in the church or trends in society, Paul Castley shows how these can become the place of encounter with God. The honest recognition of the negative can lead to faith-filled hope. This is book for slow reading and reflection.

Very Rev. Peter Slater
Vicar General
Diocese of Sale

I followed Paul's retreat program last year and found it wonderfully refreshing. With good, well-rounded pastoral experiences reflected with great compassion through the eyes of Scripture and with a good dose of common sense, this program is a real gift for the soul.

Fr Joe Caddy EV AM,
Episcopal Vicar for Social Services
Vicar-General of the Archdiocese of Melbourne.

A TIME TO HOPE

FINDING ENCOURAGEMENT IN PRAYER AND MINISTRY

PAUL F. CASTLEY MSC

COVENTRY
PRESS

Published in Australia by
Coventry Press
33 Scoresby Road
Bayswater Vic. 3153
Australia

ISBN 9780648566120

Scripture quotations are from *The New Jerusalem* Bible, copyright 1985
by Darton, Longman & Todd, Ltd. and Doubleday, a division of
Random House, Inc. Reprinted by Permission.

Cataloguing-in-Publication entry is available from the National Library
of Australia http:/catalogue.nla.gov.au/.

Design by Megan Low (Filmshot Graphics - FSG)
Cover by Ian James - www.jgd.com.au

Printed in Australia

Contents

I do not believe in coincidences. I believe in the Providence of God. I am convinced that all things are guided by a Loving God towards a glorious outcome that we call the Kingdom of God. I prefer to call it the Empire of God as the Greek word used in the New Testament for Kingdom is the same as that used for the Empire of Rome. Jesus was contrasting God's Empire with the vicious, exploitative and cruel empire of Rome that shares these characteristics with any other human empire.

This little book has its origins in several retreats. After giving such a retreat to the priests of the Port Pirie Diocese, some of them suggested that I publish them. The very next night after returning home to Melbourne, I was due to go to a concert. To cut a long story short, I ended up running into Hugh McGinlay of Coventry Press and he was interested in publishing these talks.

I am a Missionary of the Sacred Heart and I cherish deeply and fondly the spirit of my congregation, a spirit that religious congregations call their charism. Charism means gift. Our charism is the gift given to the Church by the Holy Spirit. Ours is a spirit that flows from the Heart of Christ and is impregnated with the qualities of Jesus' Heart: tenderness, affection, loyalty, courage and the ability to challenge. It is strong but it is also full of mercy and forgiveness.

The concert I went to that night was a concert version of the opera, *Thaïs*. This opera tells the story of a monk in Ancient Egypt who seeks out a prostitute and calls her to conversion. He is full of condemnation of her ways and of sexuality in general.

The irony is that Thais is converted and enters the convent but he becomes infatuated with her. Pride comes before a fall. As Jesus says, 'Don't judge and you won't be judged.'

The friend who took me to the concert remarked at half time that one of the things he found most jarring in the church was its harshness. These comments echoed what I had heard some time ago from one of my Irish colleagues, Nick Harnan. Nick had worked in England and South Africa and, when he returned to Ireland some years later, he was disturbed most of all, not by the sexual abuse scandals — horrendous and devastating and all as they were but by the harshness in the Church's attitude to people. Perhaps the harshness has the same source as the abuse: the insensitivity of some of those with power to the plight and the struggle of so many of us.

I hope the spirit of my congregation permeates these chapters and is an antidote to the spirit of harshness that so often afflicts our Church. After all, the traditional devotion to the Sacred Heart that was propelled into the modern church by St Margaret Mary was a response to the harshness of a heresy called Jansenism.

I hope that this little work will help some people to hear more clearly and respond more readily to the words of Jesus, 'Come to me, all you who labour and are burdened and I will give you rest. For I am meek and humble of heart; and you will find rest for your souls.'[1]

A Spirituality of the Heart

I have mentioned the charism of my religious congregation. A congregation's charism is that aspect of the mystery of Christ that the congregation is called to reveal to the world. Being one of the many Sacred Heart congregations, we began emphasising

---

1   Matthew 11:28-29

and spreading Devotion to the Sacred Heart. St Margaret Mary Alacoque, who lived in the seventeenth century, had been responsible for proclaiming that devotion to the then modern world.

This devotion was expressed by many wonderful prayers and practices that were suitable for such an age but, following the Second Vatican Council, there has been much more emphasis on Scripture, theological learning and sacramental practice to nourish our faith and our relationship to the Father, through Jesus in the Spirit.

In the mid-seventies and early-eighties, the Superior General of our Congregation, Father, later Bishop, Jim Cuskelly helped us adapt this wonderful devotion to modern times. He spoke of a Spirituality of the Heart.

As in the earlier devotion to the Sacred Heart, this spirituality continued to focus on a deep, personal and reciprocal relationship with Jesus. It consisted of what Cuskelly called the four movements of spirituality and I often think – in this way – it has similarities to the poem, The Heart is a Guest House, by the 13th Century Sufi Mystic, Rumi.

Cuskelly teaches us that the first movement is a movement into our own hearts to discover and honestly face what we find there: in Oliver Cromwell's famous phrase, 'warts and all'. In the second movement, we take what we find in our hearts to the Heart of Jesus. What do we find there? We find compassion, understanding, forgiveness, delight, affection, gratitude and so on.

My mention of gratitude may seem strange but I mention in the text that follows my favourite mystic, Julian of Norwich, who says that God is grateful to us.

The third movement of the heart is the hope that wells up in us when we experience this encounter with the Heart of Christ.

I have noticed that if I simply wallow in misery when I discover what is in my heart, I will sink further into misery. If I look up, as it were, and share with Christ all that is in my heart, I notice something changes in my outlook: a burdened eased and a weight lifted.

The fourth movement is a missionary impulse. I am led to go out and proclaim this good news to all the nations. Here is the Good News that gives meaning and sense to life.

I notice in the recent daily papers the tragic news of the rise in youth suicide. Many professionals attribute this rise to the meaninglessness and hopelessness that so many young people experience today.

Jules Chevalier, the founder of my congregation, said that devotion to the Sacred Heart was a cure for *Le Mal Moderne* – the evils of the modern world. A *Spirituality of the Heart* offers the same cure to all of us in this present modern world.

Introduction

I will begin by making two points. The first is to recommend a way of praying as you make time to reflect. Many people, I am sure, are familiar with it. Permeating this way of praying will be an attitude of just gazing at Jesus, of contemplating Christ Our Lord. One can start with noticing what comes into our hearts, especially during times we set aside for quiet prayer and reflection. Notice what you are feeling, what you are experiencing. It may be your joys. Memories will come flooding in and stories will abound. Perhaps these memories will be of the good you have done and will bring you enormous satisfaction.

No doubt, many of you have had experiences similar to the one I had some time ago. A woman rang me. She mentioned her name and I hadn't the slightest memory of her or any idea of who she was or where she fitted into my life pattern. She said that she'd tried to ring me two years ago but was told I was in Rome. She mentioned she'd walked into our MSC parish church in Brisbane about 1974. She saw I was reading a book called *The Power of Praise*. I vaguely remember it. I couldn't now tell you who wrote it but she knew it was written by a Protestant and the fact that it was being read by a priest was somehow liberating for her. Apparently, she had had two children in the space of 15 months and life was extremely stressful for her. I haven't any idea of what I said. Perhaps, I was one of those dubious 'easy priests'. Whatever it was that I said, it, too, was liberating. The conversation seems to have had a lasting impact on her life.

If such memories are brought to mind, notice how they affect you. Is it gratitude to God that you have had an impact on someone's life? Share that with God. Is it awe that God could work in such a way through you? Allow that awe to rise to the surface of your consciousness and share it quietly and wordlessly with God. Is there a reluctance to accept this accolade out of fear you might become vain or bigheaded? Acknowledge that reluctance and, perhaps, fear and share it quietly with God.

Perhaps God is trying to teach you something through this reluctance and free you from something, so that you might, for example, rest gently in gratitude to God for God's workings in and through you. I also love the idea of Julian of Norwich that God is extremely grateful to us for what we have done. I remember saying that to a group of priests many years ago. An elderly priest responded, 'Yes. We do need to be grateful to God.' I don't think he quite got my point. It is a bit mind blowing to think God is grateful to us.

Or perhaps other memories might come with an accompanying fear or anxiety or hurt or pain or rage – what I now call afflictive emotions. To entertain them might be hard or painful or distressing. I would urge you, though, to face them and embrace them. Then share them honestly and gently with Jesus. He does say after all, 'Come to me, all you who labour and are burdened, and I will give you rest.'[1] When someone, in spiritual direction, has mentioned a great sorrow or hurt or pain or something like that in their life and I ask them have they shared this with Jesus I so often get the reply that they hadn't or that they didn't think of doing that.

I know from my own experience and from the experience of so many after they have done this, that something like relief or calmness or a greater sense of OKness is experienced. The hurt hasn't necessarily been healed. The pain hasn't necessarily gone

---

1   Matthew 11:28

away. The cause of the anxiety hasn't disappeared off the radar, but they live now with a little more tranquillity and peace. It's not so much a petitionary prayer to deliver us from the things afflicting us. That may not be possible. It's just an exposing of our hearts to Jesus and allowing his spirit to breathe on our wounds and soothe them. I'll expand on this later when I talk about a spirituality of the heart.

What I'm suggesting ties in with a book written by Brian Gallagher MSC, who founded the Heart of Life Spirituality Centre in Melbourne. A second edition came out co-authored with Sue Richardson PVBM. It was *Pray As You Are*. Pray as you are, not as you think you ought to be. As you spend time in quiet reflection, just be yourself before God—warts and all, virtues and strengths.

The second point I'll raise is that I think in today's experience of being Church, it is appropriate to make our prayer one of lament, that is found so often in the psalms. I won't go into it here. I'll spend a whole chapter on it later on. Exiles lament. Once I use that word exile, I'm reminded of that prayer that we so often used to say, the 'Hail, Holy Queen.' It contains the words, 'to thee do we cry, poor banished children of Eve' – and the word for banished is 'exules', exiles. We are exiled children of Eve. 'To thee do we send up our sighs mourning and weeping in this valley of tears.' Beautiful stuff!

A couple of years ago, when I was preparing to use this theme of lament, I mentioned it to a very good and wise friend of mine – a layman. He urged me to make sure I spoke to priests of hope. Priests need hope. I notice that at the start of the 'Hail, Holy Queen', we hail Our Lady as 'Our Hope!' So while we'll talk later on of lamenting as a valuable Biblical form of praying, in this introduction, for just a few moments I'll jump the gun and ask you to contemplate the meeting of Jesus and the disciples on the mount in Galilee. One of the most memorable homilies I ever heard was on this subject and it was preached by an Archbishop, no less: Patrick Kelly, of Liverpool. He used to stay with the Sisters of Nazareth at Hammersmith in London and occasionally I'd meet him when I repaired there to catch up with Peter Malone, one of my Australian MSC community.

For many years, it was Archbishop Kelly's residence when he visited London. He reminded us that when Jesus appeared to them, they bowed down but, tellingly, 'some doubted.'[2] There right at the moment of commissioning, of sending out the apostles, some doubted. To people such as these Jesus entrusted his mission and his church. I have often preached on the fact that both of the foundation apostles, Peter and Paul, were men with flaws and these flaws persisted after their conversion when they were in the midst of their ministry. Peter was a coward, an impetuous, loveable one but he denied Christ out of fear.

Later on, Paul rebuked him because he let that fear of others affect his dealings with the gentile converts. He wouldn't eat with them in the presence of the Jewish Christians. Paul was a firebrand and persecuted the church. Later on he had a blazing row with John Mark and wouldn't take him with him on another missionary journey. To such flawed men Jesus entrusted the leadership of his church and the spreading of his Good News.

He could do that because he would live up to his promise made to the disciples on the mount, 'that I will be with you always even until the end of time.' Just let those words re-echo in your minds and hearts and imaginations tonight as we begin this reflection in this time of exile and lament. As we think of exile, we can think, too, of hope and trust in the promise of Christ.

---

2   Matthew 28:17

You may be embarrassed or feel uncomfortable, if not guilty, that you fall asleep when you come to pray. Years ago, I heard a very wise spiritual director say that there are two reasons why we fall asleep at prayer. One is that we are avoiding something. We don't want to face something. We don't want to think about it or be reminded of it. The other is that we need to fall asleep and we are tired. It reminds me of the phrase attributed to Freud. 'Sometimes a cigar is just a cigar'. There doesn't have to be any symbolic reference in it. The mention of a cigar may be just that – a reference to a cigar and not a Freudian slip. So tiredness may mean just that. Give yourselves the benefit of the doubt and, if you are weary, acknowledge your weariness and rest. Many of us have busy stressful lives.

Whatever space you're in, go gently. We need to keep before our eyes the Jesus who said, 'Come to me all you who labour and are burdened.'[3] This is the Jesus whose bowels were wrenched by the meeting with the leper,[4] when he realised what we humans do to one another.

I'll refer again to some of these beautiful and well know incidents in Christ's life. So I won't expand on them now. I'm mentioning them now, just to set the tone for a time of quiet and prayer. Rest, gentleness, and letting the Lord touch you with his friendship and affection – the same sort of affection and friendship he had for his disciples. They must have been tough guys. They were fishermen among other things and must have had to mix with the rough and tumble of life. They would have been physically strong and I don't know whether I would have liked to meet them in a pub brawl. Jesus liked them. He likes us.

---

3   Matthew 11:28
4   Mark 1:40-42

Chapter 1
The Loving Kindness Of God

Some years ago, I walked the Camino de Santiago de Compostela. I trudged, walked, stumbled, strode, ambled, and maybe, at times, staggered for about 1800 kilometres from Chalons-en-Champagne in France, not far from Rheims, through Vézelay, up over the Pyrenees and along the Camino Frances. Just a Sunday afternoon stroll for a 79 year old! Many people these days have followed one or other path of the Camino. When I went to the Pilgrim Office in Santiago to collect my Compostelle, the certificate that vouches for the completion of one's pilgrimage, I asked also for a Certificate of Distance.

There was a touching moment when the young woman asked how far I had walked and checked my Pilgrim's Credenciales/ Passport. She was impressed and said that of all who had checked in on this particular day, I was the one who had travelled the furthest. Then I told her I was 79. She must have told that in Spanish to the rest of the office staff and they all stood and gave me a warm ovation. Touching, and delightful, as I said, but a little embarrassing!

As I firmly believe 'breath is for walking, not for talking', I much prefer to walk on my own in contemplative silence and leave the socialising to the afternoons and evenings when one catches up with the many lovely people one encounters on the way. In this contemplative silence all sorts of thoughts tumbled around in my head. All sorts of feelings stirred in my heart, yet in the midst of what at times seemed a muddle and chaos the Spirit created space that was filled with a deepening of my understandings of God and Jesus and Mary and the spirit of the founder of my Order: the Venerable Jules Chevalier. Sometimes, the insights could be into who I really am and, on those occasions, I wasn't always elated. At times, it seemed as if I was moving from head to heart. It seemed I came to experience things, not just to know them.

I can remember the moment when it did hit me with unusual but gentle force that God did listen to my prayers. God did pay loving attention to me. It was a revelatory moment. It was a moment of amazement. I had known this, of course, but at this moment I think I experienced it at a heart level. It was a moment that could draw me into a deeper intimacy with God if only I paid attention to it.

I was fascinated by the direction my thinking and experience then took. There were lots of people on The Way. So if God listens tenderly and attentively to me, then God listens tenderly and attentively to everybody. Each one of these people is significant to God. Each one is important in God's sight. Not only has every hair on your head been counted; and not only does no sparrow fall to the ground without your Father knowing,[1] all of these companion pilgrims are known intimately to God who is more intimate to them than they are to themselves.[2] The thought moved on. God attends to all those I have seen as I passed through all the cities and villages of Spain and France. God is intimately and lovingly aware of all the people back in Australia. God has had full knowledge and tender regard for every person who has trod this earth. Each has been, and still is, important to God. Each has been the object of God's constant and affectionate regard.

---

1   Matthew 10:30
2   Augustine *Confessions* 3.6.11

My reflections took two paths, at least. Let's start with something that was a gift of God even before I started journeying. I am sure – in the providence of God – I was directed by the Holy Spirit to do some reading. I do not believe in luck or in coincidence. I believe in the Providence of God. First, I was on supply in a particular parish and I noticed Cardinal Walter Kaspar's book, *Jesus the Christ*.

He wrote that God's very nature is to bless. God wants only to pour out on us blessings. From all eternity, the Father pours out God's whole beauty and goodness in the Word and both share everything with the Spirit and the sharing is reciprocated by the Spirit. I won't bore you with a sterile lecture on the nature of the Trinity except to say that the inner life of this central mystery of our faith is one of infinite outpouring of goodness and love.

From all eternity, the Father is aware of all that infinite beauty, goodness and love. As it were there is an eternal gasp of delight and joy that is the Word that expresses all that wonder of infinite being. And from all eternity the two are wrapped in an infinite dance of love. In my day in the seminary we had those wonderful tags of scholastic (mediaeval) philosophy and theology. The one that springs to mind here is, 'Bonum est diffusivum sui'. Goodness, by its very nature, spreads itself abroad, pours itself out everywhere.

Out from the Infinite origin of all things is born everything that is. It comes to us through the Word and is enlivened by the Spirit. How many galaxies are there? Is it 200 million or 2 billion? I read the other day that there are trillions of them. Does it matter which is correct? When one deals with those numbers, each one is mind boggling. Each invites us to awe, amazement, wonder and worship. And in each of the galaxies, how many stars are there? Is it again 200 million or 2 billion? Whatever it is, it's beyond our grasp.

At the heart of all creation and at the very core of each atom is a love that sustains everything in existence. At the heart of everything, more intimate to everything than things are to themselves, is a presence of love and beauty and goodness. At the heart of everything is, in the words of the last line of Dante's *Divine Comedy*, the love that moves the sun and the other stars.[3]

When we finally gaze on this infinite goodness, beauty and power, we will be transfixed, stunned and rendered speechless by it all. We will, I am sure, experience a tremendous reverence. I take tremendous literally: the *mysterium tremens et fascinans*: that mystery of wonder that utterly fascinates us and causes us to tremble reverentially. We experience a reverential fear or respect for the mystery that engulfs us. Yet respect is too weak a word and fear doesn't sit easily. It's not a fear of something evil that will damage us. It's an awe that teaches us we are creatures and, though creatures, we are embraced and transformed by a breathtaking love.

As I reflected on this mystery of beauty and love, I was challenged by all those Old Testament and devotional expressions of God's wrath and anger at sinners that were so much the staple of fundamentalist preaching. I wonder if some fragments of these still lie buried deep in our psyches. You could think of many quotations I am sure. For example, we can turn to Joshua in Deuteronomy: "thou shalt smite them and utterly destroy them; thou shalt make no covenant with them, nor show mercy unto them."

A 16th century fundamentalist preacher, Nicholas Lockyer, quoted God's instructions to Ezekiel, "slay utterly the old and the young." Another quoted Jesus from Luke 19:27 "those mine

---

3   *Paradiso* Canto XXXIII l 145

enemies, which would not that I should reign over them, bring hither and slay them before me." In the breviary, the daily prayer book used by priests, we have readings from Joshua and Judges that are full of the slaying of Israel's enemies, seen as the enemies of God.

Psalm 106 is used in one place. It contains similar 'jewels' that reflect the scowls of a vicious God. In verses 15-18, 'God struck them with a deep wasting sickness... the earth opened and swallowed up Dathan and buried the clan of Abiram... fire blazed up against their clan and flames devoured the rebels. Phineas is commended in verse 18 for his actions.

In Numbers 25:7-10, we read he murdered an Israelite and his Midianite wife. Other horrific and grotesque acts, worthy of Islamic State insurgents in Iraq and Syria, are acts of execution allegedly ordered by God to deflect God's burning anger from Israel. For several years now I have refused to read the hymn for Holy Week that is contained in the breviary. Why? Its first lines run,

Man of sorrows, wrapped in grief,
Bow your head to our relief;
You for us the path have trod
Of the dreadful wrath of God.

There it is! What a disgustingly distorted vision of God! The Passion of Christ and its horrific brutality are seen as the consequences of the fury of a seemingly vengeful God, outraged by the crimes we commit.

It is true that there must be something in God that models our anger at the horrors and abuse we see perpetrated so often in the world. God is certainly not indifferent to what traumatises the children loved so tenderly. I write this as we come to the end of the Royal Commission on sexual abuse inflicted on children.

We are angry at the abuse inflicted on them. Surely God, too, detests that. Comments I'll make later on what God's anger is like and what its purpose is, will encompass also God's detestation of abhorrent crimes.

Fortunately, we understand that the authors of the sacred writings are heavily influenced by their ambient culture but these sorts of quotations can perpetuate the myth of an angry, vengeful God of the Old Testament who is contrasted with the compassionate, forgiving God of the New. We know this is an absurd attitude. I do not want to focus on such distortions. I do wonder, however, if some trickles of such foetid streams have seeped into our unconscious and affect our vision and our experience of God. So let us spend a little bit of time contemplating the God described in the lectionary for the first reading of Trinity Sunday Year A.

In Exodus 34:6, Yahweh passed before Moses on the mountain and Moses called out, 'Yahweh, Yahweh, God of tenderness and compassion, slow to anger, rich in faithful love and constancy, maintaining God's faithful love to thousands, forgiving fault, crime and sin.' True, anger is referred to, but in a way hugely different from the way it is mentioned in other quotations. After all, the two Hebrew words most used of God in the Old Testament are *hesed* and *emeth* – or love and fidelity, affection and loyalty, saving love and truth, or, as here, faithful love and constancy.

That's the truth about God. We need to ask ourselves: is God calling us to a deeper understanding of God's tenderness and affection, and a richer transforming experience of God's love and mercy, to the revolution of tenderness Pope Francis longs for the Church to experience?

Another piece of Kaspar's writing that had quite an impact on me before I began my walk was a statement in his book: *Mercy*.

The Essence of the Gospel and the Key to Christian Life. It's a book that Pope Francis has praised so highly. Kaspar says somewhere, 'God's Justice is not a punitive justice. It's a desire to put things right'. So even as we are horrified and angry at the tremendous evil in our world, God's attitude is not to destroy and obliterate in wrath but to put things right. If you like, God's anger is this urgency in the heart of God to bless all God's creatures – even Islamic State and Boko Haram. God doesn't want to destroy them. God wants to renew them and to restore them to a pristine goodness. God thirsts for our freedom from all the evils that afflict us.

At this moment, I'm reminded of a response of one of my deceased MSC confreres. When asked in his old age, 'Have you improved much over the years?', he responded, 'Not much. But I have learnt one thing: God loves me'. What a beautiful response!

I'd like to refer to a few passages in the Old Testament. I'll start with Hosea. As you know his wife was persistently unfaithful. Yet God urged Hosea to keep taking her back. God was imaging out in Hosea God's attitude to us. God says of Israel, 'Look, I am going to seduce her and lead her into the desert and speak to her heart.'[4] I don't know if erotic is quite the word for it. The words, 'I'll speak to her heart,' are certainly evocative. They are so intimate. They are so full of the longing of God to be in loving communion with us. They are the words of someone who breathes love, someone whose heart gently but powerfully throbs for another, as God's heart longs for us.

Another text I offer is from the 'Song of Songs.'[5]

I hear my love. See how he comes
Leaping on the mountains, bounding over the hills.
See where he stands behind our wall.

---

4   Hosea 2:14
5   Song 2:8-10

He looks in at the window, he peers through the opening...
He says to me, 'Come then, my beloved, my lovely one, come.
For see, winter is past, the rains are over and gone.
Flowers are appearing on the earth...
Show me your face, let me hear your voice.
For your voice is sweet and your face so beautiful.

I love the energy, the excitement, the breathless passion for us that is caught up in the words, 'Leaping on the mountains, bounding over the hills' like a stag. I love the image of God, 'looking in at the window, peering through the opening,' desperate, as it were, to catch sight of us, for, as it were, that is what would make God happy, just being in loving communion with us.

Just relish the words, 'Come then, my beloved, my lovely one, come.' The rhythm itself is so redolent of God's awe at the beauty God sees in us. 'Winter is past, the rains are over and gone, flowers are appearing on the earth.'[6] God wants to share all this loveliness with us. God wants us to delight in it all. 'Show me your face, let me hear your voice, for your voice is sweet and your face so beautiful.'[7] Hear God saying *that* to you, to each of us. For in each of us is a God-given beauty in which God delights.

If you feel a resistance to welcoming this, if you feel uncomfortable about letting God come so close and be so intimate that's OK. Just ask God to free you so that you can become spellbound by God's affection.

Another passage that is redolent of God's affection is Hosea 11:1-9.

'When Israel was a child, I loved him.' Here's the love of a proud father for a child. No doubt you have seen and I have seen, too, a father utterly dumbfounded, utterly amazed with love as he

---

6   Song 2:10-12
7   Song 2:14

gazes on his newborn child. Some of those reading the Scriptures will have had such an experience themselves. That's God's attitude to us. 'I taught Ephraim to walk... I took them by the arm... I was leading them... with leading strings of love.' Theses leading strings were the harnesses with which fathers used to teach their sons to walk.

I love the affection and tenderness in, 'I was like someone lifting an infant to his cheek'. Feel that! Imagine that! That is how God wants to approach us. The Israelites had ignored God and had worshipped other gods in hillside shrines. As in a cuckolded lover, the utter pain of being rejected rises up in God. God struggles with the rage evoked by the agony of spurned love. 'Since he has refused to come back to me, the sword will rage through his cities destroying the bars of his gates, devouring them because of their plots.' Love, however, triumphs. 'I can't do this. I can't allow to happen what happened in the past, "For I am God not human. I am the holy one in your midst, and I shall not come to you in anger."'

Let's go to Jeremiah 31:3. The translation I used to quote was, 'I have loved you with an everlasting love; therefore I am constant in my affection for you'. I respond with delight to the word 'affection'. It says more to me than even 'my faithful love'. It seems to clothe a word we perhaps overuse – love – with flesh and blood, with heart. We all know the tenderness of affection. It is so important that we pay attention to the times when our hearts register affection. It is so important to realise that that feeling is only a pale image, as it were, of what God 'feels' for us. I have inverted commas round 'feels' in that sentence. Perhaps I should say it's only a pale image of God's attitude to us. I think it's important that we allow ourselves to ponder these words in God's presence and allow the amazing fact of God's affection for us to touch us deeply.

There are a couple of other ones, old favourites that I'll mention. We can go to Isaiah 43. 'Don't be afraid... I've called you by your name, you are mine'. Just let that resonate in your hearts and minds. God is looking lovingly at us and saying, 'you are mine.' Let yourself hear God say that to you personally. Let it touch your heart and soul.

Isaiah goes on, 'I have given Egypt for your ransom, Cush and Seba in exchange for you'. Egypt was a great and powerful empire in ancient times and Cush and Seba were distant and exotic places, no doubt sources of spices and other fine products. Yes God is prepared to give everything for us. We are more important to God than anything else. Why? 'Since I regard you as precious, since you are honoured and I love you'.

As I walked the Camino, I thought, 'All these people I'm passing! They are all precious to God. God listens to their prayers, too.' It may not have been as powerful as Thomas Merton's experience, where he was overwhelmed in a street in Louisville, Kentucky, or somewhere, with an extraordinary experience of realising that all the people around him were precious to God, but I sensed this truth in a deeper way than I had before.

Would that we could all have such a profound experience as Merton's. Let's start first with pondering the fact, 'I am precious to you, my God'. If we let that touch us deeply, we may more easily realise how precious we all are to God. If we realise how we personally are precious to God, we'll certainly be drawn more closely to God and into a more intimate relationship.

I'm sure we have our own favourite passages in the Scriptures. Go to them. Read them slowly. Savour them. Let them seep into your consciousness and if any stains of those false images of God remain there, allow the Holy Spirit to act on you through these texts and enrich you, instead, with more accurate and appealing images of God's affection for you.

I mentioned Islamic State earlier. I imagine that we're certainly horrified at some of the atrocities they have perpetrated. Perhaps at times we feel a rage at what they have done. Perhaps it would be more illuminating to think of something that touches us more personally. Perhaps we're outraged at the treatment received by someone we love. If we weren't angry, I would imagine there would be something wrong with us. Do we want to destroy the perpetrator? Do we want to punish the perpetrator? Of course, they must be brought to justice. Do we want to approach this task in the spirit of a truth and reconciliation commission as was held in South Africa or in Timor Leste? Or do we want to approach them in a spirit of vindictiveness and revenge or payback? I guess it's a bit like the old cliché, 'Hate the sin, but love the sinner'. That's pretty hard. Some of the Old Testament texts I've quoted seem to approximate more to hating both the sinner and the sin. They seem to glory in the elimination both of the sinner as well as the sin.

I think it is good to take up the Old Testament image of God as loving Father – and indeed at times, as loving mother. The parent can be angry with the child and may seek a suitable disciplinary action for the good of the child but doesn't want to damage the child in any way. The parent is seeking only the good of the child. Kasper writes that God wants only to eliminate the evil that harms us. God does not want to be vindictive or harm us. I suppose a bit of my problem with the anger of God is that for most of us standing before a really angry person venting their rage at us can be an experience we'd all like to avoid. It hurts. It sears. If they have lost their temper, it's very hard for any good to come from that.

I'm reminded of an incident in my first year out of the seminary. I was in Randwick in Sydney. We had no computers and calculators then. Receipts for the huge number of donors to the planned giving were handwritten after the amounts had been calculated by the good old adding up of columns of figures. I'd rushed the job to get it over with. To my shame, I think I wanted to get out quickly and go to a performance of Mozart's version of Handel's *Messiah*, conducted by Sir Bernard Heinze in the Sydney Town Hall. Anyhow lots of complaints came in.

There was no rage expressed by the PP but his words, 'Bad business, Father, bad business', left me in no doubt of what he thought and felt about it all. It affected me, indeed, and was a potent inducement to a reform of morals, shall I say; but it didn't crush me. I think I did learn a lesson but till this day I have no bitterness or resentment. He was a godly man, this PP. Here, perhaps, was a wholesome image of the anger of God and how God will challenge us to do better. It won't be a crushing rebuke.

Nonetheless, I want to invite us all back to contemplating the tenderness and affection of God. I had many favourite texts and, as I write this, I recall one afternoon many years ago – nearly forty - sitting in the presbytery with a girl of about seventeen who was in the youth group. I was taking her through some of the favourite texts. A couple of years ago, I was in Brisbane and was able to attend the funeral of her mother. I was looking forward to catching up with her. From the look of her, I think she'd been down a rocky road. She looked more lined and withered than I'd expected and she introduced me to her 'partner', not her husband. It wasn't the time to enquire further.

I did bring up, however, the memory of that afternoon. I told her I had an abiding memory taking her through those passages. Her response was intriguing. It went something like, 'Father, you don't know what a lasting effect such an occasion has'. I took it to mean that she remembered the occasion, too, and that it had been influential in her life. The texts did, at the time, seem to amaze her and be a revelation to her. I suppose I quote that story to illustrate the words of St Francis de Sales. Didn't he say, 'You attract more bees – or flies – with a spoonful of honey, than with a barrel of vinegar'?

I'll go back to some of those favourite texts. For example, Isaiah 49:13-17.

> *Shout for joy, you heavens; earth, exult!*
> *Mountains, break into joyful cries!*
> *For Yahweh has consoled his people, is taking pity on his*
> *afflicted ones.*
> *Zion was saying, 'Yahweh has abandoned me, the Lord has*
> *forgotten me'.*
> *Can a woman forget her baby at the breast,*
> *Feel no pity for the child she has born?*
> *Even if these were to forget, I shall not forget you.*
> *Look, I have engraved you on the palms of my hands.*

I have an amusing memory connected with this quotation. On my ordination holiday – nearly sixty years ago – my father and step-mother took me to a Hayes Gordon production of *Fiddler on the Roof*. I'll never forget – perhaps I have it carved on the palms of my hands!!! – the wife sounding off at Topol – was that his name? – about the shopping and not to forget this and that and the cabbage and everything else. In frustration, Topol responded, 'Yes! Yes, mother! I'll never forget. I have carved them on the palms of my hand'. Perhaps it was something about the descent from the sublime context in which I'd always heard the phrase to the, if not ridiculous, at least the amusing, no doubt common, domestic situation here on stage.

At times, maybe today, we are tempted to think we are abandoned by God, as Sion did. Has God forgotten me or forgotten the Church? Has God forgotten the Chosen People? God assures us, emphatically and graphically: 'No!' Then follows that absolutely beautiful image: that extraordinary claim by God. 'Can a woman forget her baby at the breast, feel no pity for the child she has borne? Even if these were to forget, I will never forget you. Look, I have engraved you on the palms of my hand.' To carve on the palms of the hand was a Hebrew idiom asserting something could never be forgotten.

Right now, we can hear those verses in the context of the nails that tore the holes in Jesus' hands. God would go this far for us. God would never forget us. We men can't come near to comprehending what it must be like for a mother to carry a child for nine months in the womb. How can she forget that? We know, sadly, some do but they are sad, dysfunctional people. Even if that happens, God can't forget us. God cannot forget the breast feeding. God cannot forget the water and blood pouring from the heart and breast of Jesus on the cross. God can never forget the tenderness and the intimacy of God's relationship with us.

There are so many more texts. I'll just quote two more: both from Isaiah.

Here is Isaiah 35:1-4.

> *Let the desert and dry lands be glad,*
> *Let the wasteland rejoice and bloom;*
> *Like the jonquil, let it burst into flower,*
> *Let it rejoice and sing for joy.*

The glory of Lebanon is bestowed on it, the splendour of
Carmel and Sharon;
Then they will see the glory of Yahweh, the splendour of our God.
Strengthen all weary hands, steady all trembling knees
and say to the faint-hearted,
'Be strong, do not be afraid. Here is your God…he is coming
to save you'.
Then the eyes of the blind will be opened, the ears of the
deaf unsealed,
Then the lame will leap like a deer and the tongue of the
dumb sing for joy;
For water will gush in the desert and streams in the wasteland…

I was quite surprised, many years ago, when a very well read confrere of mine, whom I admired immensely for his theological learning, said that that text was describing the judgment of God. God's coming is about wastelands rejoicing and blooming. God's judgment is about bursting into flower, rejoicing and singing for joy. God's judgment and coming are about taking away our fears and steadying our trembling as we struggle along.' True, there is talk of vengeance coming and divine retribution but the final words are God saving us.

In another context, I will mention how Jesus omits from his quotations from the Old Testament and in some of his other words references to vengeance and cursing by God. He moves us on from there. That is not his experience of his affectionate Father.

Read Isaiah 54:5-10.

Your creator is your husband, Yahweh Sabaoth is his name,
The holy one of Israel is your redeemer…
Yes! Yahweh has called you back like a forsaken grief-stricken wife…
I did forsake you for a brief moment,

> *but in great compassion I shall take you back.*
> *In a flood of anger for a moment, I hid my face from you.*
> *But in everlasting love, I have taken pity on you…*
> *Though the mountains may fall and the hills turn to dust,*
> *My faithful love shall never leave you.*

Sure, there is again reference here to the anger of God, repudiating us like a very patriarchal husband, forsaking us like so many husbands we know of, but to emphasise the compassion and the affection of God towards us, Isaiah reassures us that, whatever we may think of God's initial responses to our infidelities, God cannot but embrace us with affection. What an extraordinary image! 'Though the mountains may fall and the hills turn to dust, my faithful love will never leave you'. That last phrase is the essential truth about our God.

We can end on a lighter note. I love the story told by Cardinal Basil Hume, the wonderful Benedictine Archbishop of Westminster in England. As a boy, he used to steal biscuits from his mother's pantry. One day, she caught him and said, 'You may think no one sees you; but someone does – God!' It took him years to throw off that image of God spying over his shoulder and watching every action to catch him out. 'Now,' he said, 'I think God would say, "Take two!"'

Let's ponder this essential truth about God and absorb it into our bloodstream. Our God is awesomely infinite, holding in being, by the divine presence at the heart of things, everything that exists. Yet that infinity is best expressed in tender love for each of us.

What a God we have! Let's take time to sit with that.

Chapter 2
Jesus

I invite you to call to mind a good friend you have. I hope you have had the experience of meeting someone and their eyes light up with delight. They smile because for them it is good to see you. Something happens to you, too. You're comfortable in their presence. Something true comes alive in you. You're in a better space. You are enjoying being in their company.

Have you ever experienced this with Jesus? It may be worthwhile to look at a few episodes in his life and allow them to reveal to you even more clearly his affection and friendship for you. Have you any favourite episodes of his encounters with people? Persistently urging itself on me is the post-Resurrection scene by the lake in John.[1] He's watching his friends out on the lake – fruitlessly fishing. We know the exegetes tell us that John is saying they were trying to go back to the old ways, but it wasn't working. We can keep that in mind; but I'm just inviting you to ponder, not the theological or exegetical meaning, but the humanity of it all – the loving kindness and friendship incarnated in Jesus our friend.

Just imagine you're working away somewhere and it isn't going too well. Is Jesus interested in you and your efforts and your striving? Look at him encouraging you as he encouraged the seven in the boat. Let his desire to help you, touch you. In your reflection and prayer, it would be very worthwhile to take time to share with him some of the plans you have, some of the

---

1   John 21

frustrations you experience, some of the exhaustion and anxiety that burdens you.

John was the first to recognise that it was Jesus standing on the shore. Peter, captured by one of his many impetuous impulses, plunged in and swam towards the friend he had betrayed. I'll talk later, too, about dry, emotionless, desert times when we don't have any affective experience or contentment in our relationship with Jesus. That may be true for much of our lives, but perhaps, at times, we've had something of John's knowing. We're swamped with difficulties, confused about where to go and what to do, even quite discouraged, but underneath it all we have a quiet momentary assurance. Jesus is with me; Jesus is sustaining me. It may even be more than a momentary quiet assurance. Underneath the clamour of all that afflicts us, there abides a quiet, almost unnoticed, sense that the Spirit is with us.

(My father lived till he was 97 and went into a nursing home only two years before he died because my step-mother who was an excellent nurse cared for him devotedly, even though she was in her nineties, too. I will never forget being with her one afternoon. We were in the kitchen of our family home and she was telling me how hard it was. She wasn't whinging or complaining. She was just telling it as it was. After pouring it all out, she paused momentarily and then said, 'But I know I'm being supported.' There it was: the awareness of the quiet presence of the sustaining Spirit of God!)

What a marvellous response of Peter! He'd betrayed and denied Jesus. Yet he was ready to leap into the lake and strike out to his friend. What did he see in that courtyard a few days before when, after he had three times denied knowing Jesus, his Lord turned and looked on him?[2] What sort of look engaged

---

2   Luke 22:61

him? – a look that melted his heart. He wept bitterly. It was a look that didn't crush or bruise his heart or ego. He did not weep remorsefully. He was heart-broken, no doubt, but not bound up in a destructive sorrow. It was a look of love that invited him to acknowledge his failure, take full responsibility for it, not excuse himself in any way, but then move on in trust, knowing he wasn't rejected. It was a profound sorrow that I have trampled on love and yet still been met with love.

There was no harshness in Jesus. He let his own vulnerability touch Peter. It's the sort of vulnerability we experience when we let go of resentment, the cutting remark, the retaliatory response and just experience how open we are to pain and abuse from the other. The other can respond with further abuse or can be completely disarmed by our attitude. It's courageous because when we choose our stance, we don't know what the re-action will be.

Jesus had touched Peter profoundly with that look. Again, when we're in a mess, when we're embarrassed or ashamed of our own failures it would be good prayer to stand there before Jesus just owning to him who we are and what we've done. We can be in his presence as the publican was, standing at the back of the temple.[3]

In that wonderful parable, the Pharisee, the religious person, boasted about his goodness. The despised publican or tax collector could only hang his head and beg, 'Lord, have mercy on me a sinner'. No doubt, Peter heard, when he was overwhelmed by that moment of purifying contrition, words even more reassuring than those Jesus used of the publican, that he went home at rights with God. I am sure that Peter realised he was more than being at rights with God.[4] I'm sure he realised that he was still engulfed in the heart of Christ.

---

3   Luke 18:9-14
4   Luke 18:14

In *Evangelii Gaudium*, Pope Francis calls us to be involved in the 'Revolution of tenderness.'[5] I think the next scene is permeated with tenderness. These tough fishermen, who in their day no doubt solved disputes with contentious fellow fishermen in, shall we say, unconventional ways, came ashore and were a little subdued, indeed sheepish. They'd fled; they'd let him down; they'd boasted and competed; and they'd failed. They would, at times, I am sure, have loved to have asserted their male prowess. Their bravado was all show when the chips were down. Yet there he was, getting breakfast for them. Appreciating their tiredness and their long night, he nourished them.

That's his recompense to us when we 'slink' back to him after our failures. (John McKinnon, a priest from Ballarat, in his commentary on John 3:17-18, says that Jesus' only judgment on his disciples after the resurrection is three times to say to them, 'Peace be with you!') They were slowly learning what Francis teaches us in *Evangelii Gaudium*, 3, 'The Lord doesn't disappoint those who take this risk; whenever we take a step towards Jesus, we come to realise that he is already there, waiting for us with open arms.'

The final scene in John's narrative is so memorable – Jesus' firm, gentle, manly questioning of his friend. Peter, are you totally committed to me more than these others? Lord, I'm fond of you. Peter, are you committed to me? Lord, I'm fond of you. Peter, are you fond of me? Of course, I am, Lord. You know there's no need to ask that. Of course I'm fond of you. I don't think the different words Jesus uses and to which Peter replies are what my wonderful secondary school English teacher, Tim Kelly, called elegant variations. They're more than that. Jesus uses a word for love that means total, dedicated commitment. Peter responds by

---

5   Evangelii Gaudium, 88

claiming he's very fond of Jesus. Notice how they develop. 'Are you committed to me more than these others?' That echoes Peter's boast, 'even if these abandon you, I won't.' 'Lord, I'm fond of you.' No boasting comparison here! 'Are you committed to me, Peter?' 'Lord, I'm fond of you. I can't claim unshakeable commitment. I'm very fond of you.' Jesus then uses Peter's word, 'are you fond of me?' Peter was upset. Of course I am. You know that even as you know I can fail disastrously.'

We can look Jesus in the eye, too, and be vulnerable once again and say, 'Lord, I'm pretty frail. I fail often and will do so in the future, but I want to be with you'. And we'll hear him say, 'Feed my lambs, feed my sheep'. We're in good company. As I've mentioned, one of the most memorable homilies I have heard was by an Archbishop – Patrick Kelly of Liverpool. It was in Easter week. The Gospel was Matthew's missioning on the mountain in Galilee. In the very moment of being sent by Jesus, 'some hesitated'.[6] These frail, hesitating men he trusted. He trusts us.

We could choose any number of scenes: how he was deeply moved by the plight of the leper.[7] Notice the intensity of, 'Of course I want to', in response to the leper's plea, 'If you want you can heal me'. It cost Jesus because he touched the leper. In Jesus, there was no fastidious reluctance to be intimate. Because he touched this disease ridden man, he became ritually unclean and so he had to stay out in the wilderness lest he contaminate others with what infected the leper.

Jesus loved feasting – he was accused of being a glutton and a drunkard.[8] His companions were sometimes pretty low types. Whatever we think of ourselves, he'll enjoy being with us,

6   Matthew 28:17
7   Matthew 8:1-3; Luke 11:45
8   Matthew 11:19

He was profoundly moved by the loss suffered by the widow of Nain. She had lost her husband and now her only son was dead. The 'age of entitlement' had certainly ended for her. There were no pensions in those days and her two breadwinners were no longer there to support her. We can pour out to him all our personal pain – our losses, our hurts, our disappointments. Our friend will be deeply concerned.

I've said, 'Take all our hurts to Jesus'. So often, our prayer doesn't seem to work. It may be pretty dry and boring, but if we're faithful we'll gain energy or, at least, stability from our fidelity.

What I've said so far has emphasised our personal, intimate relationship with Jesus. This is important but there's another dimension to Jesus that I'd like to highlight as well for it can balance in a healthy way a possibility of overlooking a spirituality that upholds the social and communal dimensions of Jesus' mission.

Jesus came to announce the presence amongst us of the Kingdom of God – the reign of God. I have only recently learnt that the word used in the New Testament for the Kingdom, the Reign, of God is actually the same word as was used for the Empire of Rome. On the one hand, we have Jesus proclaiming that the Empire of God is among you. God is acting to establish God's Empire. On the other hand, we have the Empire of Caesar and the petty little kingdoms that oppressed the vast majority of people. They were vastly different.

Listen to Luke:[9]

> *'The Spirit of the Lord is upon me,*
> *For he has anointed me*
> *to bring the good news to the afflicted.*
> *He has sent me to proclaim liberty to captives,*

---

9   Luke 4:18-19

sight to the blind,
to let the oppressed go free,
to proclaim a year of favour from the Lord.'

As you know, he is quoting Isaiah 61:1-2. There is one outstanding and obvious omission from Isaiah's text. Unlike the prophet, Jesus wasn't sent to proclaim a day of vengeance for our God, words found at the end of Isaiah's text. The God and Father of Jesus Christ wasn't, isn't and never has been a vengeful God, despite how often some fierce fundamentalists like to depict him. The God and Father of Our Lord Jesus Christ, 'so loved that world that God sent the son not to judge the world, but so that through him the world might be saved'.[10]

I would encourage you to listen to what he longs to do for the people of God. I know I have just said I want to look at the social and communal dimension of Jesus' mission. None the less, let's spend time hearing him say it to us, personally, that he wants to free me from what keeps me captive. We can take this announcement of Jesus as a paradigm for our Christian life. And it is! But let's hear Jesus say it to us, first. What are the addictions that keep me captive and from which I don't seem to be able to free myself. Indeed I can't free myself from them? That's why Jesus came. What are the things that bind me: the habits, the weaknesses, the vulnerabilities? Maybe I know them and, to my shame, they keep rising up to confront me despite all my good resolutions.

(I'd like to add a footnote here. Martin Laird, an Augustinian, has written a wonderful book called *Sunlit Absence*. In it he says that John of the Cross' teaches that during the Dark Night we experience 'excruciating sufferings of the intellect'. When I first read those sorts of things in John of the Cross I shuddered. Ugh!

---

10   John 3:17

I thought. I don't want to go there. Laird, however, says that these 'excruciating sufferings' are the awareness that there rises up within me so many petty thoughts and desires, so much meanness, so much harsh criticism of others.

We're aware of inclinations within us that can be very embarrassing. Perhaps many years ago we didn't realise what we were like. Now God is revealing them to us. It hurts. It makes us suffer. We're powerless to change ourselves. As we learn to peacefully accept ourselves, as we learn to acknowledge calmly and simply that that's what we're like – we are actually travelling through the dark night of the soul and are being purified by God so that we can be drawn by God more fully and deeply into God's loving embrace. Let's return, however, to the communal and social dimension of the Empire, the Kingdom of God.)

Who were the people Jesus mixed with? I've been quite surprised recently, shocked even, to realise I didn't understand the extent to which Jesus challenged the cultural, social and religious attitudes and behaviours of his day. I knew he did it extensively but I really didn't understand the enormity of his counter-cultural activity. The first shall be last and the last shall be first. In this society there were a few wealthy landowners. They lived in splendour, wealth and comfort, like the rich man, Dives, who ignored the utterly destitute, starving and diseased Lazarus at his gate, begging for a few coins to survive. When sickness affected the ability of these poor to work and grow their crops, or a bad season left the struggling small time farmers with nothing to support themselves, they needed loans. When they couldn't repay them, the wealthy man who lent them money seized their lands and drove them off their small farms.

There were two types of poor. There were those who could, indeed, eke out a living by hard, laborious work. They may have had enough to survive on and to keep at bay the worst pangs of hunger. They would have had a roof over their heads, at least. Then there were the poor who were utterly destitute. The poor were taxed by the Herods and petty rulers of the day. They were taxed by the Romans. And they were taxed by the temple treasury. They were the victims of the Rulers of the Gentiles who lorded it over them.[11] The people like Lazarus were jobless and homeless. They were diseased and malnourished.

They were the people Francis refers to in *Evangelii Gaudium*: they weren't just the exploited and the oppressed. They were excluded from society. They weren't just disenfranchised or those on the fringes. They were the 'leftovers'. [12] They were the lepers that people drove from the towns and villages because they were ritually impure. They couldn't be part of the religious or social life of the times. By touching them, one brought down upon oneself the same fate. They were like the 'ten'[13] who came to meet Jesus, but called out from afar, 'Jesus, master, take pity on us'. They'd heard of him and no doubt knew his heart had been moved by a deep seated compassion for other lepers whom he'd embraced and healed.[14] However, they kept their distance. That was their place.

They were like the blind Bartimaeus[15] whom others wanted to silence and with whom the others did not want to be associated and whom others wished to prevent coming in contact with Jesus. They were those standing idle in the market place all day because they'd lost their land to the greedy landowners who built bigger barns[16] with crops produced on land wrenched from these poor

---

11   Mark 10:42; Matthew 20:25; Luke 22:25
12   E.G. 53
13   Luke 17:11-19
14   Matthew 8:1-4; Mark 1:40-45; Luke 5:12-16.
15   Mark 10:46-52
16   Luke 12:16-20

debt-ridden erstwhile farmers.[17] To the amazement of his hearers, no doubt, Jesus called these wealthy ones, 'Fools'. He cast his lot with others. They were the utterly despised women who were so poor and so without hope that the only way they could survive was by turning to the ignominy of prostitution. These people were the poor, the crippled, the blind and the lame who lived in the streets and alleys of the town[18] or who were at the main crossroads, the open roads and the hedgerows[19], the good and the bad alike[20] whom the father of Jesus Christ wanted at the banquet. The only places these people had to live in were on the open roads and sheltered only by the hedgerows.

Jesus was passionate about those standing idle in the market-place. Like his Father, he passionately wanted them to be paid the day's wages so they could be fed, no matter what time they were hired. Even the terms sinners and tax collectors have greater force than I imagined.[21] The sinners were not those who didn't observe the law because they couldn't understand its complexities. They were the ones who deliberately lived outside the Covenant. To them Jesus came with the Heart of his Father with the Good News that they were welcome at the table of God. They were the lost that he sought out. [22]The tax collectors weren't in charge – the wealthy who made much of being appointed by the Romans. The ones with whom Jesus ate were petty, disreputable and dishonoured men, often slaves, who have this shameful occupation of sitting in collection booths and gathering taxes at transit points, like bridges, ports and highways, leading out of towns and villages. One of the

17   Matthew 20: 1-16
18   Luke 14:21-24
19   Luke 14:23
20   Matthew 22:9-10
21   Pagola ch 7
22   Luke 15: 4-7

greatest disgraces of the prostitutes was not so much their sexual activity but that they entertained the hated Romans.

Years ago, when I was in Brisbane, I received a call from a man who called himself Mr Robinson. I loved that touch, Mr Robinson. I assume he was battling to hang onto and assert something of his dignity. He wanted a handout. I told him to come to the presbytery as he wasn't far away. I don't think I've seen too many people as grubby as Mr Robinson. I thought he was wearing black socks but I realised that he wasn't. His ankles were so dirty that it just seemed he was wearing black socks. The black stretched unbroken from his shoes up his trousers. I gave him something and he reappeared a few more times. Then one morning he turned up at breakfast time. Our formidable housekeeper came into the dining room and informed us that there was 'a dirty disreputable gentleman at the door'. She wasn't at all happy when I asked her to give him some sandwiches. Looking back now, I should have done it myself. It was these dirty, disreputable people with whom Jesus associated.

In Jesus' time, one ate only with those you respected and who would bring you honour if you were seen in their company. Jesus invited all these disreputable and dishonourable people to his table. In the face of all, he offered them his respect and reminded them of their dignity, a dignity with which no one else would credit them. As Luke 7:35-50 shows, us the wealthy didn't invite prostitutes to their table. They were shown no respect and accorded no dignity. Yet Jesus defended the woman and contrasted her love and her behaviour with that of the so-called honourable man.

If we can understand how low on the social scale these people were, if we can understand how degraded they were and with what contempt they were treated we can begin to understand the amazing attitude of Jesus to all of us and how passionate the Father is about the welfare of all of us.

They were so often homeless and malnourished. Jesus lived amongst them. The fact that his disciples ate the wheat on the Sabbath indicates that, at times, they, too, were hungry. That Jesus said he had nowhere to lay his head[23] indicates he had taken up a lifestyle like theirs. He cast his lot with the homeless. He urged his disciples not to wear sandals; nor to provide themselves with gold or silver or even coppers. Have no haversack, or staff or spare tunic or footwear.[24] Slaves wore no sandals, only the masters of the house. (I know the different Gospels have slightly different accounts of what they were to take; but the principle was the same.) They'd cast their lot in with the homeless outcasts of society, who didn't have these things. They stood in total solidarity with the lowest and most vulnerable of all. This was the way of the Father.

This was the new thing God was doing in Jesus: offering the fullness of blessings to anybody and everybody. No one was excluded from the empire of the Father. And the poor flocked to it. For once, they'd met a prophet who didn't discriminate against them. They'd met someone who showed them the unbelievable magnanimity of God. In Christ, they knew that God hears the cry of the poor.

Jesus, the incarnate son of God, can do only what he sees the Father doing.[25] What he sees the Father doing is discriminating against no one;[26] offering love and the fullness of life to all. There's no Pelagianism[27] here. God doesn't wait for us to merit anything.

---

23   Matthew 8:20; Luke 9:58
24   Matthew 10:9-10; Luke 9:3; Mark 6:9
25   John 5:19
26   Matthew 5:45
27   Pelagianism is a heresy that says we have the power to merit from God. We don't. All is gift.

We can't! We can't merit the transforming union of love with the divine that raises us up to an incomprehensible level of life and love. Jesus just wants to bless good and bad alike.

He shocks his disciples by telling them it's an absolute impossibility to be a citizen in the Empire of God, the Empire of love and self-giving, if we serve Mammon.[28] The last will be the first and the first, in their reckoning, he calls fools.

We could look, too, at his attitude to women. The last in their patriarchal society will be the first. No longer is it the woman who is blamed for the adultery. No longer is she the temptress, the lascivious one, the seductress. No longer is she the one who is dragged into the open and shamed and threatened by the patriarchal society.[29] She is not condemned. It's the men, those who have the first place in the Empires of this world, who are challenged about their innermost, adulterous thoughts and drooling looks.[30] It's the women, too, who are the first to experience the Resurrection and sent as the first messengers of the Good News to the men who at first don't believe.[31]

The point I'm trying to make is that Jesus gazes at each of us with immense affection even if we're down and out, lowly, without skills and success and have failed miserably or experience our weakness to the full. When we're in strife and all our plans have come to nothing, he's still there with us supporting us. He seeks us out when we're lost, because, as I've said, God wants only to bless and give life and life to the full.[32]

---

28   Matthew 19:24; 6:24
29   John 8:1-11
30   Matthew 5:28
31   Matthew 28:1-10; Mark 16:9-11; Luke 24:1-11; John 21:1-2,11-
      18
32   John 10:10

Chapter 3
He Is Risen

In 1986 and 1987, I was stationed in Drummoyne, Sydney, where for many years my religious congregation had a formation house. I was the director of our students' pastoral formation. One fellow used to visit the residents at the Little Sisters of the Poor up the street from us. Regularly, the students had to present written accounts of the pastoral situations in which they were involved and of their meetings with the people to whom they ministered.

One student was presenting his account of a conversation he had had with a sprightly old lady. She was energetically bustling around, getting him a cup of tea and telling him her life story. She had been widowed many years and, I think, had also lost a child quite a long time ago. I was jarred by the student's attempts to bring her back to these incidents and his attempts to explore her grief. He was portraying her as quite a lively and bright old lady. At last I asked, 'What were her eyes like?' 'They were bright and shining', he said. Even his lit up when he said that and his voice became a little excited too. 'Precisely', I responded. That description was certainly congruent with the bustling and energetic way she was going about things and with the seeming delight she had in his visit.

Even I, once removed from the encounter, found her liveliness contagious. So I asked, 'Has it ever occurred to you that she's done her grieving?' I think here of Elizabeth Kubler Ross' work on the grieving process in which having passed through pain, anger, loss and such like, one comes eventually to a calm acceptance. I'm sure, of course, if one has had a beautifully loving relationship there will always be a hollow place in the heart but not such that it prevents one from rising to a new and blessed life. It is carried as a healed wound.

I wouldn't be surprised if, from time to time, you felt a bit downcast and a little despondent if not depressed if you remember friends and relatives who are in pain from the degenerative processes of age. I rang my eldest brother recently. He's 87 and in answer to my enquiry about how he was going, he was able to admit to a few more aches and pains but that he was going well. He certainly seemed quite bright but was more concerned with his wife's pain.

She had just had some surgery and it hadn't all gone quite right. Though he was well, he was, naturally, affected by his wife's pain. I would imagine, too, that we all often provide a listening ear to people's tales of sorrow and loss and see how weighed down they can be. Sometimes, such accounts can bring to mind our own sorrows and losses or touch into spots in our own hearts and we can be filled at times with despondency.

Then there are the whingers! I think I have said that I find whingers very hard to bear. I am reminded of when I was in Jerusalem and a Canadian priest with me asked me what 'wingies' meant? He had read a letter in *Ha Aretz* – the Jerusalem English-speaking newspaper. He said the author was obviously an Australian and he talked about 'wingies'. He couldn't understand what the letter writer was talking about. It took me a minute or so to realise he was trying to pronounce 'whingers.' If I come across someone who is constantly whinging and complaining and criticising, it takes me a while to throw off my own despondency that the other has touched. I can then start looking at the other with compassion and begin thinking, 'How sad to have a personality like that! What's he or she been through and suffered to have such a miserable outlook on life?'

Genuine compassion for the suffering, sickness, loss and sorrow of the elderly is not to be despised. It's a beautiful human characteristic. At the same time it can be painful for us, too, as we contemplate the other. It can be another notification of the pain of this world and the sin of this world and of all that can make life so horrid and miserable for so many people.

As a healthy antidote to this sorrow and not as denial, as avoidance and as repression of our pain, I think it is important we revisit the Easter scenes. We need both to contemplate them again and again at the appropriate times and to have some small but effective strategies to challenge the downward spiral of our spirits and of our hearts.

I noticed during one Easter week that there would seep into my mind some images and memories of the atrocities occurring world-wide, especially in the Middle East. It wasn't balm for the soul. Nor did I think it just quite right on Easter Monday morning to continue to dwell on these things. Sometimes such thoughts can be temptations from the spirit that is not of God. They can be undermining the work of God's Holy Spirit that is gifting us with a more beautiful faith in the victory of Our Lord Jesus Christ over sin, death and all the evils of this world.

We don't yet grasp it in full. It hasn't yet pervaded our whole being, as it will when we gaze on the splendour of God and bask in the warmth of God's love in eternity. Yet such faith and hope need to be part of our armament and, as it were, the weaponry we take into battle with the forces of darkness:[1] truth as a belt, uprightness as a breastplate, the shield of faith to quench the burning arrows of the Evil One.

---

1   Ephesians 6:10-18

When I am supervising people's ministry or listening to them in spiritual direction, I often think that quite unconsciously, when confronted with evil and disaster, they do not grasp that salvation has been won and that redemption is ours. Their mood is a darker one than just wholesome sorrow or pain. They are not listening to St Paul's injunction, 'Do not grieve as those who have no hope'.[2] There is a grief that is accompanied by hope. It's so wholesome, so humanly good and so appropriate at the right time; but I wonder if Easter week is the right time.

I cannot tell God what to do, of course. After all[3] 'Who has directed the Spirit of God, what counsellor could have instructed him. Whom has God consulted for enlightenment, for instruction in the path of Judgment, to teach God knowledge?... God's understanding is beyond fathoming.' God can summon us to enter with Jesus into his Passion and Death at any time that seems suitable to the Divine Wisdom and plan but most of the time, indeed in the vast majority of times, another spirit is required of us in Easter Week and when we are contemplating the Resurrection. If we are accustomed to listen to the whisperings of our hearts, we may notice a gentle urging - and it will always be gentle, for God is not a spirit of clamour and noise to those who are seeking God[4] - to move from the Passion to the Resurrection.

One Easter week, as I was lured into thinking of the horrors of the world, a strategy I spoke about came to mind. Into my mind came gently and unobtrusively the wonderful words, 'This is the day that the Lord has made. Let us rejoice and be glad at it'. The words themselves aren't really gentle. They urge us to celebrate with vigour. They have a rising inflection and a rhythm that quite

---

2   1 Thessalonians 4:13
3   Isaiah 40:13-28
4   Cf Ignatius Loyola: Rules for Discernment of Spirits: Week 2: 7

rightly sweeps us along with the meaning of the words. We do exult in them. As we quietly and slowly murmur these words, our spirits will respond to the invitation of God's Holy Spirit to embrace that wonderful truth, 'Jesus Christ IS risen from the dead, alleluia, alleluia!'

The truth and joy of the Resurrection become an even more integral part of our life and faith. They become more and more the dynamic that propels our life forward and enables us to radiate more and more to others that joy of the Easter Season, that joy and peace that the world cannot give.[5] 'I give you my peace that the world cannot give.' It will be a peace that becomes more and more the stable and irremovable substratum that is never washed away even if we feel overwhelmed by the torrents of misery and pain that can seem to engulf us. It is quietly whispering to us and sustaining us despite all the tempests that batter us.

We are those who have built our house upon rock. 'Rain came down, floods rose, gales blew and hurled themselves against that house, and it did not fall: it was founded on rock.'[6] It was founded on the rock that is Christ Jesus risen from the dead. We have drunk from the spiritual rock that is Christ Risen.[7] As Julian of Norwich says, 'He did not say, "Thou shalt not be tempested, thou shalt not be travailed, thou shalt not be diseased". He said, "Thou shalt not be overcome."' We think, too, of her marvellous words, 'All shall be well and all shall be well and all manner of thing shall be well.' And why is all this: because, as we have said, 'Jesus Christ has risen from the dead, alleluia, alleluia'?

I knew a wonderful a wonderful priest from Bendigo, Maurice Duffy. In an intellectually deadening context, he was in

---

5   John 14:27
6   Matthew 7:24-27
7   1 Corinthians 10:4

the vanguard of catechetical renewal and had suffered considerably for his progressive attitudes. Maurice sang in a choir we'd put together at a priests gathering at the Hume Weir, many years ago. Another priest, a Dutch White Father, commented on how happy he seemed. He asked me to introduce him to Maurice. In response to this priest's comment about his happiness, Maurice said, 'Jesus Christ is risen from the dead. Your sins are forgiven, Alleluia! Alleluia! That is what I live by.' I have never forgotten that moment.

Let's look at a couple of post-resurrection scenes. I love the one in Matthew 28:1-10. The women are up early, such is their devotion to the one who has made such a difference to their lives, who has made them equally disciples as the men. According to Mark 16, they have come with spices to treat with love the dead body of Jesus in a manner that he deserved. But he's not there. The angel tells them he is risen and then authorises them to bring the Good News of the Resurrection to the disciples.

It's important to notice that these women are the first bearers of the Good Tidings. They are the first to announce the Resurrection. They are filled with awe and joy. That joy is a constant theme in the resurrection scenes. So is awe or uncertainty. Notice, however, there is no hesitation with the women, whatever reaction is evoked in the men. They hurry off but, on their way, they see Jesus coming towards them. I think it's worth noting what happens because of their belief. Jesus so frequently said to people, 'Your faith has saved you'. It's as if Jesus is taking the first step. He is coming towards them. He's like his Father in the parable of the prodigal son. The Father doesn't wait for the son to come up to him. He sees the son coming in the distance and he rewards this faith by setting out to rush towards him. He pours out his affection on the son.

I have always been moved by the simple words Jesus speaks to the women. It's just, 'Greetings,' or 'Hello!' But I've always imagined the greeting was delivered with a rising inflection, full of delight to see his dear friends again. Hullo! Hullo! In the theological idiom of the time, they do fall at his feet and worship him. They are drawn to recognise the changed status that now envelops him. He is no longer the dusty traveller on the roads of Galilee. He's no longer only the dear friend, just being one amongst them. No, he is the risen Son of God but he carries it off in a quiet way. He comes not with trumpets blasting, legions escorting him and cavalry prancing before him, as did the Roman Generals and Governors of the time. No! He comes simply and affectionately for God's whole nature is to be affectionate. He comes like the one in Philippians 2; the one who did not grasp at his state but the one who was eager to empty himself to be of service.

The authority is quietly exercised, 'Go and tell my brothers and sisters…' what they are to do. I always experience a calmness and tranquillity of spirit as I imagine this scene. How different from the tumult of the preceding three days. He is full of joy at seeing his faithful friends. He is delighted to take the first step to discover himself to them. Sure, they came towards dawn, but on their own they couldn't find him. He had to reveal himself to them. He had to come to them. I can imagine him smiling at them, at their faithfulness and at their affection and loyalty. It's interesting that affection and loyalty – the *hesed* and the *emeth* – are the two most significant qualities attributed to God in the Old Testament. These women have been graced abundantly with them and they are filled with the divine life.

I cannot determine how you are to view this scene. That is up to the Holy Spirit's inspiration in you. The extent of my remit is only to suggest an idea or two. So, unless you are firmly drawn in a different direction, I would encourage you to look at Jesus smiling with delight. Imagine him smiling with joy at seeing you. Let him touch your heart in that way. It will deepen in you the realisation you already have of the depths of affection for us that fill his heart.

The silly old blokes, if it is not irreverent to call them that! At least twice[8] they refused to believe. In fact, in Luke, the disciples dismiss the women's story as pure nonsense. He suddenly appears among them in the upper room. Their first reaction is alarm and fright. When they see his hands and his feet, their reaction is quite extraordinary. 'Their joy was so great that they could not believe it, as they were dumbfounded.'

There is the mention of joy again. We can pray for that joy because I think it would be an indication of our affection and love. (While I say that, I want to recall to your minds the talk about darkness and dryness in prayer when Jesus does deprive us of any sensible delight in our prayer so that we might deepen our faith and hope by committing ourselves to him even when there seems to be no reward and no consolation.[9] We soldier on, as it were, because of the commitment and generosity of our wills.) This joy of the disciples in this scene is an unbelievable joy.

I suppose we are so used to the story of the resurrection we can tend to take it for granted. Just remember how unbelievers even today regard it as myth, fairy tale and hallucination. It is astounding. What would it have been like for us to be there lost in sorrow, fear and in the shattering of our dreams? How we would have gulped at the sight of this seeming apparition, at the sight of what seemed to be a ghost. Perhaps, that could be a grace we ask for – to be stunned by the wonder of it. The more stunned

8   Mark 16:11; Luke 24:11
9   See chapter 6: The Emptiness of Prayer or When the Wells Run Dry.

we are, I am sure the more it will transform us, the more it will inspire us and drive us on in our following of Jesus and in our commitment to the people we serve. Perhaps, as we insert ourselves into the scene, we will be warmed by the sheer loveliness of it all, the quiet delight of hearts and the excitement that bubbles up within the group.

Another beautiful story is that of Mary Magdalene at the tomb.[10] I noticed that though Peter and John race off to explore the empty tomb and that John sees and believes, there is no record of them at that moment seeing Jesus. Mary Magdalen has been and has gone back to tell the disciples. She doesn't yet realise what's happened. Imagine the distress and longing in her heart for this man who has shown her such understanding and compassion, who was the first man not to hold her past against her and to despise her for it. What an ache. So she goes back to the spot. She doesn't expect the extraordinary. 'They've taken my Lord away. I don't know where they've put him. You're the gardener. Have you done it? Show me where it is. I need to make sure he's respectfully buried.'

Just imagine the beauty and the affection in the tone of Jesus' voice. Who could capture it? 'Mary!' As Jesus said earlier on,[11] 'The sheep that belong to me listen to my voice'. How she had noticed all the inflections of that voice as day after day she listened to him, breathing out in his words the unbelievable love she sought in so many other different places and not found until she first was touched by it a few years previously. 'Master!' she cried and threw herself at his feet. She wanted to hold on to her treasure and not let it go any more.

---

10   John 20:11-18
11   John 10:27

She didn't want to lose it again, but she had another task and she would find him, not in holding on in deep satisfaction, but in letting go and in service – the service of telling the brothers and sisters that he was ascending to his Father and his God, to their Father and their God. That's a lesson for us, too, isn't it? It is in our service of others that we will find our God. In your ministry, you can find and embrace Christ your beloved. Perhaps it would be a good exercise to imagine Jesus just quietly and slowly saying to you over and over again your own name. It will help, I am sure, to deepen your appreciation of the affection Jesus has for you.

I have another favourite post-resurrection story. It's in John 21:9-14. Jesus has stood on the bank of the shore, perhaps on a little elevation. Like any bystander and observer, he has pointed out a shoal of fish to them that they could not quite see from their perspective in the boat at sea level. They had been so devastated by his death that they were going back to their old ways.

They were in the night. They were going back fishing. They'd forgotten they were being called to fish for people and gather them into Christ's net and into the Empire of God. They might have turned back but Jesus wasn't going to let them go. Jesus brought the light, the new dawn. He was the Hound of Heaven pursuing his loved ones wherever they tried to flee. He went after them. They were thunderstruck by the catch and John instantly recognised who the stranger was who had called out to them. As at the tomb, John realised the truth revealed by where the garments lay. Peter didn't. When he communicates his insight to Peter, the belovedly impetuous one, despite his recent failures, jumps into the water and swims towards the Master he loves. He then takes over his leadership role and goes back and drags the net to shore.

The next few strokes of the pen describe a scene that is so full of unstated care and affection. When the seven who've gone fishing come ashore, they notice that there was some bread there and a charcoal fire burning and some fish on it. Does it take you back to your childhood times and the taste of fresh bread and succulent fish? What a smell must have wafted on the breeze and delighted their senses! Just breathe it in and imagine it. Isn't it such a beautiful manifestation of Jesus' thoughtfulness and kindness? Look at how he cares for his friends even though they have only a day or two ago abandoned him to his fate.

It's the sort of treatment he wants to offer us, despite everything. I am amused at what I think is the embarrassment felt by the disciples and hinted at in the words, 'None of them was bold enough to ask, "Who are you?"' They knew it was the Lord'. I can imagine they were pretty sheepish. Apart from John, they'd doubted the women - at least I'm assuming John came more quickly to faith than the rest of them – and now they could not but believe what they had seen and at whom they were now looking.

Of course, the story works on two levels here. It becomes Eucharist. It is Jesus who nourishes them, these famished fishermen, famished for the bread of daily life but also hungering for the life of God communicated through the Eucharist. Jesus takes both the bread and the fish and hands it to them. Jesus serves them. He performs a simple ordinary ask. He feeds them. Yet that is what Eucharist is about isn't it? It's about service. Your daily lives are so Eucharistic. Not only do you receive the Eucharist when you receive Communion, when you celebrate the Eucharist with others. You are filled with the life of Christ and nourished by the life of Christ when your life is lived in service to others. You are that tender Christ squatting by the charcoal fire preparing this simple but delightful meal for his friends.

It has been pointed out to me[12] that only twice in John's Gospel is a charcoal fire mentioned. One is here; the other is in John 18:18 when, in the courtyard of the High Priest, Peter disowned Jesus. Is Jesus saying, 'You may disown me in the night, but the sun will rise and dispel the darkness and I will keep feeding you, when the sun is risen'?

I love the *Agnus Dei*. 'Lamb of God! You take away the sins of the world.' The Greek word for sin is *(h)amartia*. It means, to miss the mark. Our faith tells us that anything in this creation – physical, natural, moral, emotional and so on – that misses the mark, will be taken away, will be healed. We can travel through darkness and disasters and evils but we will eventually pass into the glory of God. 'Though I walk through the valley of darkness, no evil will I fear. You are there with your crook and your staff. With these you give me comfort…Surely goodness and kindness will follow me all the days of my life. In the Lord's own house shall I dwell for ever and ever.' Psalm 23 is such a wonderful prayer. It is good to make its verses a mantra to be gently repeated. As we gaze on the risen Christ, as we contemplate his victory over sin and death, let's remember that victory, too, is our destiny. He's leading us along that path. We will rise with him to Glory.

---

12   By Kevin Matthews of Port Pirie, when I gave this talk to the priests of Port Pirie.

Chapter 4
Reason To Hope

Some time ago, I was involved in a lively discussion at a meeting of Teams for Married Couples (Teams of Our Lady). While acknowledging that the church must honestly admit to the crimes some of our members have committed, they were deeply upset that very few were getting up and preaching about the good things that the church does. One couple commented on such a homily that they'd heard a short while ago. Their cry was, 'Why aren't we hearing more like that? Why aren't our leaders saying more in the church's defence?'

I think I was caught up in my own thoughts and really wasn't listening to the hurt in their hearts. One fellow did, indeed, try to make the point that Jesus didn't go round boasting of what he had done. We're following Jesus in quietly going about doing good things.[1] I complimented him later for his stance. He very generously said of the others that he could understand where they were coming from. It's hard to keep quiet when your team, your side, the outfit to which you belong and which has given you so much, seems to be unfairly attacked or attacked in an unbalanced manner.

I didn't think it would be helpful to repeat what I'd heard Francis Sullivan saying a year or so ago. Francis is well known as the head of the Church's Truth, Healing and Justice Committee. He told a meeting of the Leaders of Religious Congregations in Victoria that people just aren't listening to the Church and the

---

1   Acts 10:38

strategy developed by his team is, first, to keep admitting serious crimes have been committed, we made serious mistakes in the past, we apologise profoundly for the terrible hurt inflicted on those who have been abused and we are working hard to get protocols and procedures right.

The idea behind focusing on this apologetic mode and, at first, only on this is that if people hear this often enough, they might start believing a little bit more that this group is serious. They might start listening a bit more. Then, when we think the time is right, we can start putting forward the good things. People by this time may be ready to hear what we've got to say. I hope this strategy works.

Now that the whole horror of sex abuse of minors is being revealed in so many other organisations and that people can see it is endemic in our culture and not linked only to the Church, I have a sense that attacks and reports in the press are becoming less frequent. I hope I'm right. I was talking some time ago to a communicant Catholic who knows Barney Schwartz well. Barney, of course, was the Religious Affairs editor of *The Age* and wrote quite a lot on the issue and in a way some might think was biased. He says Barney is a very fine fellow. I think he showed his even handedness when he wrote a fine front page article in praise of last year's Bishop's Statement on Social Justice.

There have been some silly international statements by ecclesiastics defending the Church. Some seemed to blame the victim. Perhaps it is true that some of the attacks may well be motivated by bigotry and hostility. Some arise out of ignorance. I don't think it serves us well to flee to those sorts of refuges. It is much more truthful and honest to admit we have done shameful criminal things for which there is no excuse. I think we need other approaches. Most especially do we need to show our concern for victims by our actions.

In this chapter, I don't want to focus on this issue; but when my friends were crying out their hurt, sadness and disappointment, there was coming into my consciousness an idea that had been playing around in my mind for some time. In 2 Timothy 3:12, we read, 'Anyone who tries to live in devotion to Christ is certain to be persecuted'.[2] Now there may be some bigotry in the attacks and in the investigation and revelation of the crimes; there may some 'schadenfreude' relished by those who are highlighting the Church's failures.

I wonder, however, if we are in touch here with some deeper and more profound spiritual realities. For all its warts and failures, and for all our warts and failures, the People of God is trying to live in devotion to Christ. The author of the Ephesians says, 'It is not against human enemies that we have to struggle, but against the principalities and ruling forces who are masters of the darkness in this world, the spirits of evil in the heavens.'[3] (After originally writing this article, I read in a *Saturday Age* Barney Schwartz' article on John Allen's book about the persecution of Christians throughout the world.[4] We are the most persecuted group in the world and each year far more Christians are killed for their faith than any other group in the world.)

Down through the ages, the Church has had its martyrs. I shudder at the horror of the savagery and the cruelty that have been inflicted on our brothers and sisters. How did they survive?

There is in the back of my mind the story I heard, as a child, of the monks of the Charterhouse in London marching,

---

2   2 Timothy 3:12
3   Ephesians 6:12
4   *The Age* Nov 2nd 2013

singing, to Tyburn gallows, during the reign of King Henry VIII. I have heard tales of the seeming peace that finally descended on some martyrs in their torments. Surely, the power of the Spirit of God is active in them in these moments, transfiguring the Church with the Glory of God. I believe there are stories of the gruesome crowd who witnessed the excruciating sufferings of the poet Saint Richard Southwell, as he was hanged, drawn and quartered. They were deeply affected by his suffering and courage and cried out for a speedy end to the brutality.

We most probably will never be called to that level of witnessing to Christ. Often, I hope I never am. I think my prayer would repeatedly be, 'Father, if you can, take this chalice from me'. I think Pope Francis exposed once again his endearing personality by expressing a hope that if someone assassinated him, he hoped they'd do it quickly, as he didn't like pain. I share those sentiments.

Nonetheless, we are disciples of Christ and I think it may help if we hold in our consciousness the words of Jesus in Mark.[5] 'If people want to be disciples of mine, they must renounce themselves and take up their cross and follow me. Those who wish to save their lives will lose them. But those who lose their lives for my sake and the sake of the Gospel will save them.'

I know in the past; I have heard people seek refuge in such a quotation and claim they are being unjustly treated when indeed they deserve what they get. I'm not trying to do that. We need to hold both together: the fact that we have failed and the fact that we will suffer for following Christ. There are powers of spiritual darkness that are opposing the in-breaking of the Empire, the Kingdom, of God.

So that may be one place to stay in prayer, from time to time. When we are feeling down and depressed at what we are

---

5   Mark 8:34-37

going through at present, it might be important for us to spend time gazing at the crucified Christ and acknowledging that, 'Yes! I am there with you right now'. It may be an Agony in the Garden experience where the pain or the dread is not taken away but through this prayer, we become more centred, a little more calm and we may experience the same resolution as Jesus did when he was able to say to his disciples, 'Get up! Let us go! My betrayer is not far away'.[6]

We carry on then not through grit and resolve and the clenching of our jaws, but through the energy and clarity provided by the Spirit of God. I think it's good to keep reminding ourselves, 'Lord, I'm committed to following you. So I surrender to this present Passion of ours. I'm committed to taking up your cross and following after'.

It would be good to meditate on a few other texts as well. Let's recall the text in Matthew,[7] 'And look, I am with you always; yes, to the end of time.' Some time ago, I read Paul Collins book, *The Birth of the West*. At the end of the Dark Ages before the rise of Christendom, so often Vikings looted and destroyed monasteries, raped nuns and murdered monks. There was so much political chaos and ecclesiastical corruption. Priests were so often uneducated. Yet somehow the People of God continued their pilgrimage in faith and holiness and again and again continued to be the light of the world and the salt of the earth.

Out of all that blossomed the high Middle Ages and the theology, the spirituality, the architecture and the vibrant life of the church that came with them. (I'll insert here an expression of my amazement at such wonderful mediaeval treasures as the Cathedrals of Burgos and Leon that I contemplated on my recent Camino. In

---

6   Mark 14:42, Matthew 26:46
7   Matthew 28:20

future I'll challenge anyone who talks of the unenlightened middle ages. The architectural skills and the engineering skills needed to build such places are incredible. The craftsmanship exhibited in all the adornments is staggering.)

Even before that, despite all the destruction and the appropriation of monastic lands by powerful thugs, monasteries kept alive the culture and wisdom of the past and became great fountains of missionary activity, taking the faith to the then known ends of the earth. God was with the People of God even in its dark time. Jesus is still with us, faithful to his promises and to his love.

Sometimes I ponder with sadness the fate of the churches of Asia Minor and of North Africa. These were once thriving Catholic centres. They were destroyed or reduced in size and impact. Yet the light of faith went out to the West. From there it has spread round the world. Not, of course, that we want to base our hopes on size or power or status. I think my friends the other night wanted the church to have power and influence and regain its status and credibility.

Many are mourning today that we have lost our political influence; we have lost our status and credibility. Perhaps that is the place we should occupy, the place occupied by our crucified master. I did try to point out how this little flock survived in the Roman Empire and, despite the horrific persecutions, infiltrated the whole of society and changed its heart and mind and soul.

Paul's words to the Corinthians come to mind.[8] 'Consider, brothers and sisters, how you were called; not many of you are wise by human standards, not many of you influential, not many of you from noble families. No! God chose those who by human standards are fools, to shame the wise; God chose those who are weak by human standards, to shame the strong, those who by

---

8   1 Corinthians 1:26-28

human standards are common and contemptible – indeed those who count for nothing – to reduce to nothing all those who count for something.'

What I'm talking about here is not optimism. Optimism, as you know, is a human quality. Great and all as it is, it either arises out of one's temperament or is based on facts that can guide our calculations about the probability of a good outcome. Optimism is a wonderful quality. As some wit said once, 'Optimists are as often wrong as pessimists, but they're twice as happy'.

What I'm talking about here is hope. And hope is a virtue. It's based not on human probabilities but springs from our trust in a faithful God, a God who will fulfil the divine promises. As I've said a number of times already the two great qualities attributed to God in the Old Testament were *emeth* and *hesed* – truth and love, or as I hear Frank Andersen naming them: affection and loyalty. They are beautiful words, beautiful qualities: affection and loyalty. They are such human descriptions of God: descriptions that come within the ambit of our experience. God's truth is God's fidelity to the promises made to God's people. God will live up to them. God will be loyal to us. Christ will be loyal to us. That's why we have hope: for that reason and that reason only.

There are some other scenes in the New Testament that would be good to contemplate.[9] One is the storm on the lake. Let's first go to one of the psalms:[10]

> *Some sailed to the sea in ships to trade on the mighty waters.*
> *They have seen the Lord's deeds, the wonders he does in the deep.*
> *For he spoke; he summoned the gale, raising up the waves of*
> *the sea.*

9   Matthew 8:23-27, Mark 4:35-41, Luke 8:22-25
10   Psalm 107:23-30

Tossed up to heaven, then into the deep, their soul melted
away in their distress.
They staggered, reeled like drunkards, for all their skill
was gone.
Then they cried to the Lord in their need and God rescued
them from their distress.
God stilled the water to a whisper: all the waves of the sea
were hushed.
They rejoiced because of the calm and God led them to the
haven they desired.
Let them thank the Lord for his love, the wonders God does
for us all.

I live with Peter Malone. He is a man of many parts. For years he taught introductory course to Old and New Testaments at Yarra Theological Union. Out of that came his book, *The New Testament in the Light of the Old*. I think he would regard this psalm as the template for the story of the Storm on the Lake. The Lord God saves so many people, including those who go down to the sea in ships. In Jesus, the Lord, the same power is manifested to the believers.

We're familiar with the image of the Barque of Peter; we're familiar with the use of this story as a call to faith. In times like this, I think it's good to go back to it, again and again. The synoptics all use the story; but I like especially the touch that Mark adds to it. Matthew and Luke have the disciples crying out, 'Lord, (or Master), save us we're lost.' Mark adds their fearful cries, 'Do you not care?'

For me, it highlights two things. First of all: an awful doubt is creeping into their relationship with Jesus. They've walked the highways and byways for quite a while now. They have certainly experienced his challenges, but they've also experienced his friendship and affection. They've seen how he cares for people: how the widow, the orphan and the stranger in their midst have been objects of his outreach. He's sought the company of those with no place in society, the rejected, the abused and the marginalised. He's enjoyed eating and drinking with them, so much so that he's been accused of being a glutton and a drunkard.[11] He's enjoyed company of these close friends, too, chosen them especially from the crowds that followed him. And yet, once more, they begin to doubt. I'd imagine that, from time to time, we can identify with that. We can be afflicted with doubt and a tendency to hopelessness and the depressive experience that accompanies such a temptation.

The second point I want to comment on is, for me, a little more touching. They are starting to doubt his care for them. They are starting to doubt that affection and loyalty he extends to them as individuals and as a group. I think it would be good to spend time reminding ourselves that Jesus has a great affection for us. I like the use of the word 'affection'. I hope it doesn't sound too sentimental. I hope it doesn't grate against men's sense of their masculinity or that it's out of place in our self-awareness. For me, it is a very human word. I can use love and commitment; and they're very good words. For me affection comes right out of the heart. It's strong and it's gentle. It's tender and it's delicate. It is, as I just said, very, very human.

I'm reminded, here, of some of the contents of Julian of Norwich's *Revelations of Divine Love*. The human person realises it has got itself into a filthy mess.[12] It turns to Jesus, who is treated as 'Jesus, Our Mother.' That might be a bit startling and I won't here go into some New Testament Johannine studies that support

---

11   Matthew 11:19; Luke 7:34.
12   *Revelations of Divine Love*, Chapter 62

that. Also I need to mention that in this spot Julian is referring to personal sin and not to crises in the experience of the people of God. Nonetheless, Mark's question, 'Do you not care?' challenges us to ask Jesus, 'Are you fond of me?', 'Are you fond of your people?' Julian's writings emphasise so beautifully the care that Jesus has for us.

I like to repeat often that we all know the famous words of Julian, 'All shall be well and all shall be well and all manner of things shall be well.' In another place[13] Our Lord promised, 'I did not say you would not be tempestered, (i.e. suffer from tempests) I said, "You will not be overcome."' I do think it would be good spending time, face to face with Jesus, as it were, and asking him to reveal his attitude to me and to his people.

It won't take away the difficulty that engulfs us. It won't take away the pain or the hazard we're in. We'll still be in the midst of these. Yet something will strengthen within us. I believe we'll be empowered to go forward.

I think we could look, too, at some of the Easter scenes. Think of the appearances to the women.[14] They experience awe but also joy. He greets them simply. I love some of the other scenes, too, in the upper room.[15] The apostles are there hiding out of fear. He appears. They, too, are overcome with awe, even though Luke adds that they still can't quite believe it. On each occasion they are filled with Joy.

If we share our doubts and our fears and our downheartedness with Jesus, something like this will be given to us, too. We may have to battle to hang on to it. As we've seen from Matthew, too, the disciples had their ups and downs of hesitation, doubt

---

13   *Revelations of Divine Love*, Chapter 68
14   Matthew 28:8-9; John 20:14
15   John 20:20; Luke 24:40

and faith. We may have to choose again and again to focus on thinking faithfully.

I think it good to look at Peter's experience.[16] When he saw Jesus walking on the water, he wanted Jesus to prove himself as it were. 'If it's you, Lord, tell me to come to you'. He heard the summons, 'Come', but he grew afraid at the wind and the waves and he started to sink. Peter believed and he doubted. He went through the vicissitudes we experience. Jesus rescued him. He's with us now in all the present crises.

Come back again to Matthew 28:20. Some still doubted when they saw him on the mount of Galilee. So we're not being too bad if, from time to time, we are troubled with doubt and worry about the Church and the present crises. Each time we are afflicted, it would be good to turn again to Matthew's final words, 'I am with you all days, even to the end of time'. What a wonderful way to end the Gospel. We have reason to hope. It's an almighty challenge, isn't it? But we have time now to spend contemplating the promise of Jesus.

---

16   Matthew 14:22-33.

Chapter 5
A Time To Lament

When I first began to cobble together these thoughts, I was running them past a well-educated and deeply committed friend of mine. As I have mentioned, he reminded me that I need to offer priests hope. That was the context of the previous chapter.

I have no memory where the idea came to me about the value of the prayer of lament. I can remember being alerted to the theme by a Uniting Church minister who, many years ago at Heart of Life, was doing our Part-Time Siloam course for the formation of spiritual directors. She spoke about the psalms of lament. We'll look at a couple of them.

To say this is a time of lament and that we may need to spend some time reflecting on that may evoke an anxiety in some of us. I hope to allay very quickly anything like that. Someone once said to me that the prayer of lament was merely looking backwards and that it doesn't allow us to move forward. On the contrary, it frees us to move forward.

I think, too, that from whatever perspective one views the modern church and the direction we think it is or has been going, we will find the prayer of lament very beneficial and it will open up our hearts to the inspiration of the Spirit and to the gentle leading of Christ.

On the one hand, some of us may have thought the direction after Vatican II undermined what we loved about the Church. We may have feared that it had succumbed to all sorts of New Age, post-modernist and secularising trends. Some feel the sorrow and grief of believing they are losing the Church they loved and in which they grew up and which nourished and enriched them so beautifully. We lament and grieve over what has happened. We are fearful of the future.

On the other hand, we may assert that the Second Vatican Council opened up on a wonderful panorama but 'restorationist' tendencies have stifled the movement of the Spirit. My eldest brother was a long standing friend and close associate of Fr Ted Kennedy in Redfern. Ted exercised a prophetic ministry to the Aboriginal community of Redfern, an inner Sydney suburb. In an email some time ago, he mentioned that Ted often warned there'd be a backlash against Vatican II. My brother was hoping we're now into a 'backlash against the backlash.'

Here we have a different perspective. In spiritual direction and in general pastoral listening, I have met quite a number of people who were excited by Vatican II and were filled with hope and enthusiasm. Now their hopes are dashed and their spirits have sunk. Disappointment and even disillusionment have taken hold of their souls. But I also notice that they don't take their grief and sorrow and pain to God in prayer. They seem to have no way of dealing with their emotional responses.

Yet again I have heard priests who aren't necessarily way out 'progressives' lament that they've tried this and that and the other. They expended energy and hope in all sorts of ways and into all sorts of things and seemingly got no-where. All sorts of people in the church are lamenting the aging of our congregations, the declining numbers, the absence of the young, the lack of the influence of the church, the decline of belief, the seeming dying of the church, 'the end of Christendom', as Archbishop Mark Coleridge has put it, and so on.

These reflections and musings lead them, also, to sadness, depression, and even despair. There's an ache and a pain. What they have loved and that to which they have given their lives, their love and their energy seems sick and fading away. It isn't what it was. Some don't know what to do. Others want to return to the past and restore the status quo, as I mentioned above. Others want to retreat into a ghetto and barricade things up behind the fortress walls. Others seem to want to be aggressively condemnatory of all that is going on in this 'secular' world.

There are many different attitudes and approaches to our present situation. I can remember being very impressed, even moved, by some words of Timothy Radcliffe, the English Dominican, who some years ago was the Master General of his order. He was at one of his Order's General Chapters in Poland. He heard men passionately espousing quite contrary hopes for the Church and quite contrary fears. They were so earnestly advocating diametrically opposed policies and plans. What he also noticed was that both sides passionately loved the Church.

I think it was beautiful that he could see beyond his own views and look deeply into the hearts of his brothers and empathise with them. He could acknowledge their genuineness. In the book I was reading, he didn't say where he stood on the issues raised nor did he criticise some for holding different opinions. He could see sincere human beings deeply affected by modern events in the Church. He empathised with them. He allowed himself to be moved by their passion and pain and to acknowledge that.

I will add here that to empathise with someone is not the same as agreeing with them. I witnessed a wonderful example of that the other day. Somebody was telling me how they usually challenge strongly someone with opposed views or a seemingly less robust approach to life than the one they embrace. On two occasions, this person listened. On the one occasion, the person with opposed views appreciated the respect shown and was also willing to listen. On the second occasion, when he would have urged the other to grow up and get on with things, he held back and said rather, 'That must have been tough for you.' As a result they had a much more fruitful discussion. Yet the other person knew precisely where the narrator stood.

I can remember a young fellow many years ago telling me how much he thought of Buddhism. I felt like arguing and demonstrating what I thought, without listening to him. I held back. After a while, I was able to tell him what I found in my relationship with Jesus Christ. Because I had listened to him, he was prepared to listen to me. I don't know whether it influenced him in any way. But it was clear to him that, though I respected his statement, I didn't agree with a lot of what he said.

When we empathise, we acknowledge the emotional experience of the other. We don't necessarily agree with their opinions and ideas. We can get a sense of their pain or sorrow or fear or whatever even if we don't think their grounds for feeling that way are valid. While we think their thinking is quite fallacious, we know their emotion is quite genuine and real. We know it's useless to say that there's no need to feel that way. We need to look with them at the thinking that gives rise to the feeling. When Timothy Radcliffe was in Australia some years ago, he mentioned in a talk that if we listen to others, they will often begin to listen to us.

So wherever we are on the spectrum of attitudes to the Church of the day and to its leadership – recent and present – an appropriate spirituality or, if not a spirituality, a way of prayer, is one of lament. Let's have a look at a few biblical examples. My favourite one is Lamentations 3. It might be worthwhile to read the whole of this chapter. I'll just take a few verses:[1]

> *For me he (Yahweh) is a lurking bear, a lion in hiding.*
> *Heading me off, he has torn me apart, leaving me shattered.*
> *He has bent his bow and used me as a target for his arrows.*

> *He has shot deep into me with shafts from his quiver…*
> *He has broken my teeth with gravel, he has fed me on ashes.*
> *I have been deprived of peace, I have forgotten what*
> *happiness is*
> *And thought, 'My lasting hope in Yahweh is lost'.*

> *Bring to mind my misery and anguish; it is wormwood*
> *and gall!*
> *My heart dwells on this continually and sinks within me.*
> *This is what I shall keep in mind and so regain some hope:*
> *Surely Yahweh's mercies are not over, God's deeds of faithful*
> *love not exhausted;*
> *Every morning they are renewed; great is God's faithfulness.*
> *'Yahweh is all I have,' I say to myself, 'and so I shall put my*
> *trust in God.*

I believe that Baruch, Jeremiah's secretary/scribe, wrote this. The context is he is sitting in the ruins of Jerusalem after the devastation wrought upon it by the Babylonians.

What has happened here? He has recounted the horrors. But there are two ways of recounting horrors and groaning and grieving. One is, as it were, to look down and naval gaze or recount our woes to someone who just colludes with us and reaffirms how horrible things are. 'Yes, things are horrible, aren't they? Things are terrible.' 'Those people have done horrible things, haven't they?

---

1   Lamentations 3:10-13,16-19, 21-24

Those people are stupid and their opinions have done a lot of damage to the Church.' One just agrees with what the other has said and doesn't enter into a supportive relationship with them. The misery and the woe and the despair are compounded and there's no light at the end of the tunnel. All is gloom.

The second way is to look up to God, as it were. I'm careful of using that phrase these days as someone recently challenged my cosmology, wondering if I thought God was up there! What I say now is, 'Take your lament to God. Take your lament into your relationship with God.' That's what Baruch does here. He tells what miseries God has inflicted on God's people. Though he is not addressing God explicitly, he is relating all of his horrifying experience to his understanding of God. He has God in mind and is not just howling to the moon.

As we lament in relationship with God, we open ourselves up to God's Spirit and what does God do in the secret of the prophet's heart? God leads him to a place of hope. Notice those beautiful words after so much lamenting:

This is what I shall keep in mind
and so regain some hope:
surely Yahweh's mercies are not over,
God's deeds of faithful love are not exhausted;
every morning they are renewed;
great is God's faithfulness!
"Yahweh is all I have", I say to myself
and so I shall put my trust in him.

He starts with an outpouring of his miseries and the disasters that have swamped him. He's attending to God's role in it and God leads him to a place of incredible hope. He may not be experiencing less grief, pain or sorrow; but he is suffering less. He's arrived at some kind of emotional stability and some sort of calm. He's moved from despair to hope. His relationship with God is deepened.

Let's look at Psalm 22. It begins with the well-known words put into Our Lord's mouth by the gospel writers.

> *My God, my God, why have you forsaken me?*
> *The words of my groaning do nothing to save me.*
> *My God, I call by day, but you do not answer,*
> *at night, but I find no response.'*

> *'Many bulls are encircling me…*
> *Lions voracious and roaring open their jaws at me.*
> *A pack of dogs surrounds me.'*

On and on he goes, and begs Yahweh for help. Then what happens? Because he has opened his heart to God and has expressed to God his sorrow, rage, fear, anxiety or whatever, God can lead him to a place of calm. 'I shall proclaim your name to my brothers' (I hope to his sisters also!), praise you in the full assembly.' Then he calls on all to revere and praise the God of Jacob. 'Of you is my praise in the thronged assembly.' His sadness and grief and pain may not have lessened but something has happened to his spirit. God has touched him and led him through the pain to a place of calm.

If we express our agony, fear, anxiety, confusion or whatever to God, we will find ourselves in a different spot. At the very least, we will have the strength and courage to cope with what's happening but, even more, we shall find ourselves with the energy to begin to do something about the situation.

Psalm 69 is another psalm used by the evangelists when writing of Christ's passion. It begins:

Save me, God, for the waters have closed in on my very being.
I am sinking in the deepest swamp and there is no firm ground.
I am exhausted with calling out, my throat is hoarse,
My eyes are worn out with searching...

It is for you I bear insults; my face is covered with shame.
I am estranged from my kinsfolk, alienated from my own
mother's children...

You know all the insults, the shame and disgrace I endure...
(how apt for these days of the sexual abuse crisis.)
Insult has broken my heart past cure...
To eat they gave me gall, to drink, vinegar when I was thirsty.

The psalmist then gets angry and vengeful.

May their own table prove a trap for them, their abundance
a snare...
Vent your fury on them; let your burning anger overtake them.

What happens as he pours out his heart? How does the psalm end? Not in despair!

I will praise God's name in song,
I will extol him by thanksgiving...

The humble have seen and are glad...
for God listens to the poor...

For God will save Zion, and rebuild the cities of Judah...

The descendants of his servants will inherit it,
and those who love his name will dwell there.

He pours out to God his grief at the woes he is suffering. He expresses to God his anger and hate. Note that all this is addressed to God. It is not just vented on his enemies. The psalm ends beautifully with a message for us: 'For God will save Sion and rebuild the cities of Judah.'[2] If we pray this way, as we see the destruction of the temple of God that we love; if we pray this way and see the dismemberment of the Body of Christ – the temple of God in which we are stones set for the worship of God and a holy priesthood for the offering of spiritual sacrifices[3] - I think we will be able to reach the spot the prophet Haggai reached:

I am with you, Yahweh Sabaoth declares; and my Spirit is present among you. Do not be afraid! For Yahweh Sabaoth says this: a little while now and I shall shake the heavens and the earth, the sea and the dry land. I shall shake all the nations and the treasures of all the nations will flow in and I shall fill this temple with glory, says Yahweh Sabaoth... the glory of this temple will surpass that of the old... and in this place I will give peace.[4]

(Vaughan Williams' *Dona nobis pacem* is a choral work on war. It begins stridently and harshly but as it works through the succeeding movements, it does come to a place of hope in God and of peace. The Haggai quotation is one of its movements. Ironically, another movement in it is a fragment of a speech made in the House of Commons. My old choir master thought it would be the only speech of a politician put to music!)

What a wonderful expression of confidence! We may think things are crumbling. In fact, they are; but they are not disintegrating. Yahweh may be allowing the ripping down of

2   Psalm 69:35.
3   2 Peter 2:5-6.
4   Haggai 2:5-9.

the present structure; but Jesus, the Christ, will be faithful to his promise: 'And look, I am with you always; yes to the end of time.'[5]

I'd make a guess that all the pain and sorrow of the psalmist hasn't been taken away; but in pouring it all out to God he has opened his soul to the action of the Spirit and the Spirit has led him to a place of praise and hope. When we pray the psalms that lament about Jerusalem or Zion or the Chosen people, we can imagine we are praying about and celebrating the Church and the people of God. In the above quotation from Psalm 69, if we replace the words 'Zion' and 'Judah' with 'Church', our prayer has a present relevance.

Let's reflect on the massacre of the innocents by Herod. It's like something Islamic State would do. Matthew takes us back to Jeremiah 31:15. Matthew quotes only the section about lamenting and weeping and about Rachael weeping for her children. My understanding is that if a biblical writer quotes just one verse, he wants to remind you of the whole section. After saying Rachel is refusing to be comforted, we hear the voice of Yahweh saying 'Stop your lamenting. Dry your eyes; for your labour will have a reward… there is hope for your future after all' and so on. Again the lamenting enables us to hear God's invitation to hope. If we pour out our laments to God about the present state of the Church and the World, God will lead us to a place of praise and hope even if we still feel the agony.

This word brings us to Jesus and his agony. How did his prayer begin? 'Father, I don't want this. Take it away. Father, if it be thy will, let this chalice pass from me.' Three times he went to his prayer that night in Gethsemane. Three times he had to express to his Father his preference: what he wanted and what he wanted to avoid. Three times he had to face the horror of what faced him.

---

5   Matthew 28:20.

Three times he had to face his fears, his dread, his anguish. Three times he had to share it with his Father. Only then could he rise up with courage and an ability to face the abyss. 'Get up! Let us go! Look, my betrayer is not far away.'[6] Notice the energy of, 'Get up! Let's go!'

Notice the path along which his prayer took him and where he ended up. He faced the darkness. He entered it. He didn't apply any narcotics to it. He shared it with his Father. And his Father led him into a calmer spot. Shall I call it that? Or shall I call it a spot in which resolve triumphed over fear? He now knew the next step to take and he was able to take it. (I'll come back later to this point about waiting for the next step to be revealed.) Even then his inner struggle wasn't over; but he'd begun the journey through the horror into the light.

Again the demons assailed him. On the cross, he descended further into the darkness of the spiritual night. He went where we often feel we are - in a place where God has abandoned us. He had again to embrace his anguish. Notice that on the cross he refused the narcotics.[7] There is only one way to go: as someone in supervision once said to me, 'You mean, the only way round is through?' 'Yes!' is the only answer. He tasted the sponge that was offered him in a gesture of courtesy and then refused to let it dull his fears and feelings of hopelessness.

He cried out to his Father his anguish. 'My God, my God why have you forsaken me?'[8] He entered into a relationship with his Father. What was the outcome? His Father led him to a place of life-giving surrender. Into the space in his heart created by the pouring out of his experience in prayer, in the expression of what

---

6   Matthew 26:46
7   Matthew 26:47-50.
8   Matthew 27:47

he was going through and what he was enduring, the Father was able to enter and lead him further and creatively into the mystery of redemption. Jesus was now empowered to cry out, 'Into your hands I commit my spirit.'[9] He was able to pour out his Spirit on the newly formed community of the church standing at the foot of the cross: his mother, Mary, the beloved disciple John, his Mother's sister, Mary the wife of Clopas and Mary of Magdala.[10]

Jesus shows us the way. He accepts the reality; faces and embraces it; shares his mood, his feelings and his experience with his Father. That's the saving moment. He's now not on his own. The Father is now his companion on his journey through his present Hell. 'You will not leave my soul among the dead.'[11] If we approach the present time in this way, God will lead us through.

I'll bring up another element of the spirituality I'm proposing. In his *Lead Kindly Light*, Blessed John Henry Newman writes - (isn't it great that he will be canonised soon!!!) -:

Keep thou my feet; I do not ask to see
The distant scene;
one step enough for me.

I was not ever thus, nor prayed that thou
Shouldst lead me on:
I loved to choose and see my path; but now
Lead thou me on.

We love to be in control of things. We want to be able to direct things from go to whoa. I believe that, not only does God ask us to enter into the darkness as the only way to come to the

---

9   Luke 24:46; John 19:30
10   John 19:25-27
11   Psalm 16:10

light, God asks us all also to surrender entirely to him. Instead of clinging on to our plans, God wants us to empty ourselves in another way and leave a space which God can fill with divine inspirations and divine plans.

We're called to be receptive. That is a feminine characteristic not easy for men and especially for men in a woefully patriarchal institution. I am by no means advocating an abandonment of responsibility for thinking and planning and trying out new pastoral initiatives. I am trying here to respond to what I often come across: the anxiety that, whatever we do, nothing seems to work; the burden we carry for the responsibility to make things happen: to restore the fortunes of Israel.

It's a burden that weighs many of us down. We collect statistics and data. We rack our brains trying to analyse them. We agonise over how we can respond. And to no avail, it seems! We descend further into sadness, despondency, depression and, maybe, even despair. In this place of lamentation, we will find our God, even though that place is dark and painful and we don't relish going there. When we surrender our need to control the process and our need to predict the outcome we'd like to achieve, we'll find that God will lead us, here, too.

We want to succeed, don't we? We're tempted to think we're worthwhile when we do that. What sort of failures are we when we can't stop the rot? When we let go of that need to succeed; when we empty ourselves of that, we'll find we have created a space that can be filled now with God's inspirations. While it's painful, even fearful, to let go of our desires for control and success, we'll find we're much more peaceful.

God will come to us, but, as Newman reminds us, we can advance only one step at a time, and because we can't see the final result, we'll really have to be discerning that this is the next step we're called to and we'll have to journey with enormous faith and trust. We may need, also, to be resigned to the fact that the changes, the growth, the new thing God is creating will come after our lifetime.

I think it would be good to read the last chapters of Isaiah. I love the passion, the intensity, the urgency of 'Oh that you would tear the heavens open and come down.'[12] God assures us, 'Look, I am going to create new heavens and a new earth and the past will not be remembered and will come no more to mind. Rather be joyful, be glad for ever at what I am creating, for look, I am creating Jerusalem to be "joy" and my people to be "gladness." '[13]

As I said, I am not advocating sitting back on our haunches and not doing anything. I am suggesting that if we really lament, we will discover God. If we make space for God's inspirations by surrendering our needs for control and success, we'll make space for God's plans to be poured into our hearts and to illuminate our minds and energise our wills.

It's a painful way of embracing our darkness and anxieties and fears and the grief that the present causes us. Paradoxically, though, we'll walk in hope for we've emptied our hearts of our desires and given space for God to fill them and we'll know what the author of the Book of Revelation knew:

Then I saw a new heaven and a new earth: the first heaven and the first earth had disappeared now…I saw the Holy City, the New Jerusalem, coming down out of heaven from God, prepared as a bride dressed for her husband. Then I heard a loud voice call from the throne,

'Look, here God lives among human beings.
God will make his home among them;

---

12   Isaiah 64:1.
13   Isaiah 65:17.

they will be God's people,
and God will be their God.
God will wipe away all tears from their eyes;
there will be no more death
and no more mourning or sadness or pain.
The world of the past has gone. [14]

---

14   Revelation 21:1-4.

Chapter 6
The Emptiness Of Prayer
or
When The Wells Run Dry

Previously, we talked a bit about how we could pray. I suggested that for some of us it might be a time of lamenting at the state of the world and the state of the church. I've added the state of the world because on the morning of the day I started writing this chapter, I was disturbed by stuff in the newspapers. There was an article on calling for a new paradigm for the way we fight drug trafficking in the world. There was another on the amount of corruption in Indonesian society and the army. It was very depressing.

Many years ago, I heard Helder Camara tell us that he prayed out of what he read in the newspapers. Helder Camara was the prophetic Bishop of Recife in Brazil who lived simply and pursued justice for the oppressed. I have been very fortunate to have been able to listen to men like Jim Cuskelly, former auxiliary bishop in Brisbane, and before that the superior general of my religious congregation, the Missionaries of the Sacred Heart. More fortunately, for me he was, in the seminary, our lecturer in ascetical theology, that is: the theology of the spiritual life. Though he didn't give us the technical name for it at the time – at least I don't recall he did – he described to us John of the Cross' *Dark Night of the Senses*.

He disagreed with the interpretation put on it by such eminent writers as Garrigou-Lagrange and Tanqueray who, at that time, were regarded as the world experts in this area and whose textbooks were used in the seminaries of the day. For years, when my prayer didn't seem up to much, I just remembered Jim saying that this is normal and that this is how it will be for most of us for a long, long time. He also quoted regularly the English Benedictine Dom John Chapman whose letters on spirituality were wonderful. Chapman would say, 'Pray as you can; not as you can't.'

Brian Gallagher is another near whom I've been fortunate to be for many years. The title of his own book *Pray as You Are* mirrors the words of Chapman and its content urges us to take account of what we're experiencing and thinking and feeling as we come to prayer. If we're in a joyful, grateful mood, then pray out of that. If we're in a sad, frightened, anxious state, then pray out of that. Let our prayer begin where we are, not where we think we should be.

Once again, I want to say, you have most probably discovered already your own personal way of praying. This is where spiritual direction is so helpful. We can think we're on the wrong track. Our prayer can feel pretty useless, empty, barren, with nothing going on and we can be tempted to quit. We may just be on the right track but don't realise it. I can remember commenting to Brian Gallagher once about a couple of our fellow Missionaries of the Sacred Heart who really didn't understand what was going on in their prayer and they had either given up or thought they had. I can't remember what the first one said but the second said, 'I don't pray any more; I just walk in the presence of God'. Then he hastened to add, for he was a profoundly spiritual man, deeply respected by those to whom he ministered, 'I don't have set times.

I just walk in the presence of God.' I told him that that was a most profound way of prayer. Obviously, he had not given up on prayer, he just didn't realise that God was calling him to a deeper form of prayer. And I would say that, quite as obviously, he must have spent plenty of time in quiet with his God, to keep nourished this constant sense of the presence of God.

I remember Brian saying how sad it was that they weren't in spiritual direction. They could have begun to understand better what was happening to them and where God was leading them. As I said, you may have discovered your own way already. If it seems right, stick to it. For example, there's been a lot of work done on Lectio Divina these days. There's also been a lot of work done by the Christian Meditation Movement. Others have found their source of prayer in the methods of the Charismatic Renewal.

I'd just like to insert here a paragraph from the Office of Readings[1] for the Optional Memorial of St Romuald on 19 June. It goes, 'He was so often carried away in his contemplation of the Godhead that he was overwhelmed by tears. Then, in the burning ardour of divine love, he would cry out, "Beloved Jesus, my beloved, my most sweet Lord, desire beyond all telling, the joy of the saints, the delight of the angels," and other similar phrases. It is impossible for me to express in human language all that he would pour forth in sheer joy under the inspiration of the Holy Spirit.' (When I quoted this to a group of priests some years ago, they burst into laughter. One of their number was named Romuald.)

The quotation reminds me of the words of a very funny but very cynical priest with whom I once lived. The old form of Readings in the breviary was called Matins. On major feasts, there were three nocturnes each composed of three Psalms followed by three readings. The second nocturne was a life of the saint with all

1 A section of the Priests' Prayer Book

its old fashioned pietistic exaggerations. This priest said the French had a *bon mot*, 'You lie like a second nocturne'.

Nonetheless, I do not want to disparage such descriptions, like those about St Romuald. We all have our times of God given consolation when we can feel fervour; when it's easy to pray and we're prompt in committing ourselves to the building up of the Reign of God in our midst.

But often enough, our prayer is pretty dry. St Teresa of Calcutta experienced most of her life an excruciating absence of God. Somebody once said to Thérèse of Lisieux, when she was suffering intensely, something like how consoled she must be to know that God loved her so much. Therese's response was, 'God is a big black empty nothing'. Our prayer experience and life experience mightn't be that dark but prayer can be dry and often there's a tug to be somewhere else. It takes a real commitment and a real choice to continue on. We can be discouraged, fearful and not experience a lot of comfort.

Perhaps we learnt to pray first by learning by rote those staple prayers: the Our Father, the Hail Mary, the Glory Be to the Father, the Hail! Holy Queen and so on. I suppose many of us were then led to pray in a discursive way. That is, we were taught to take the Scriptures and read them and reflect on them. We'd think a lot about them. We'd work out how they applied to us and what lessons we could draw from them. We'd been taught that then we'd make acts to God – praise, thanksgiving, worship, sorrow and petition and so on. That served us well for a while but then, perhaps, things didn't seem to be working.

We were dry. We were in the dark. Nothing was terribly satisfying. We didn't seem to be getting anywhere and perhaps we gave it away or we went along in fits and starts. When we felt good, we began with zeal again but then as the dryness came along, we thought things were going wrong again and we slacked off again. For all the exhortations we'd heard about the necessity of prayer, we found it pretty dull, dry, boring, and dissatisfying. There must be something wrong.

For many years of this off and on sort of approach to prayer, I was sustained by Jim Cuskelly's words that that was how it was going to be. I thank God for them. Though I would have from time to time slacked off, in general I kept coming back to spending, at least some time most days in prayer. My mantra was more, 'Well, this is how Cus said it would be,' rather than, 'Jesus, Son of the Living God, have mercy on me, a sinner'.

Then, in 1993, I had to take over giving a seminar on 'The Human Experience of God' that Brian Gallagher gave to the people doing Siloam. (Siloam is a program for the formation of spiritual directors run at the Heart of Life Spirituality Centre, Melbourne.) I looked at his notes and realised I didn't have the confidence to do it and indeed I most probably had neither the requisite knowledge nor the talent to do it. So it was suggested that, over the fourteen weeks the two hour seminar was to last, I take a different mystic each week, get the participants to read, prayerfully reflect on the material and then share their prayerful reactions on what they'd read. Each week, I'd furiously read as much as I could of a chosen mystic, photocopy a significant amount and hand it over to them. I was definitely like the teacher who kept one class ahead of his pupils. My confidence wasn't helped when one with missionary experience in the tough areas of Mexico asked what help John of the Cross would be to him on his mission station in Mexico.' I could answer him now. I couldn't then.

One wonderful lesson for myself that I drew from them was that a very basic Christian experience is that 'I am a loved sinner'. The thunderous judgments of a harsh God were not the staple food for Christian growth and the following of Christ. Neither was a sense of the angry God. We are sinners, indeed. Actually, I don't like that word as it has, for me, overtones of all that fundamentalist preaching. Be that as it may, we do need gently to acknowledge our weakness, our frailties, our failures and our brokenness; but we have to accept our state in the light of an extraordinary love, a love that was manifested in Jesus welcoming the prostitute, the tax collector and all who had failed in one way or another. That is the way he will welcome us. I am reminded of Pope Francis' words in *Evangelii Gaudium*, 'Every time we return to Jesus, he welcomes us with open arms.'

From two of the selections I drew another lesson. The two were *The Cloud of Unknowing* and John of the Cross' *Dark Night* and his *Ascent of Mount Carmel*. I started to realise that what was happening in my prayer was what was being described in these books. One very helpful saying in the *Cloud* was that 'Your distractions will be your cross'. Are they ever! I think that may resonate with your experience. The author's basic premise is that God cannot be grasped by thought but only by love. That's pretty orthodox theology.

Note, as I said above, when we began to pray, we were taught to think about and reflect on a passage of Scripture. The author keeps saying 'There is a Dark Cloud of Unknowing between us and God. It can't be penetrated by thought only by love.' 'Pierce the dark Cloud of Unknowing with darts of love.'

That troubled me for a while as I was looking at Love in a very affective way. Love is, of course, basically an act of the will. Quite a while ago, a French-speaking person helped me on this point when he pointed out to a group that French has two words for love: *amour* and *charité*. *Amour* is the affective one. *Charité* refers more to commitment of the will. The author is virtually saying, 'Hang in there. Choose a mantra and when the distractions come, just return to your mantra, whatever you feel'.

Perhaps you've had the experience, not only of distractions, but also that the old way of praying and reflecting just didn't seem to work. You may even have felt that you didn't want to take the Scriptures and read them. I'm not advocating, of course, that we stop reading the Scriptures. We need to go back to them again and again. The gospels, the psalms, the prophets are rich and nourish us with new insights or deeper convictions. Each night, for example, I love to say Psalm 134

> *Come, bless the Lord, all you who serve the Lord,*
> *who stand in the house of the Lord*
> *in the courts of the house of our God.*
> *Lift up your hands to the holy place*
> *and bless the Lord through the night.*
> *May the Lord bless you from Sion,*
> *God who made both heaven and earth.*'[2]

My spirit gives a little kick, as it were, at the thought of blessing the Lord. My point here is that we do need regularly to be nourished by the Scriptures. Yet my experience was that for quite a while when I came to prayer. I felt like putting the book aside, I felt like ceasing to reflect on it and just wanted to be there. I was plagued for a while with the thought that I was being lazy; I didn't want to put in the effort; I just wanted to take an easy way out. There was nothing much in my mind and precious little in my feeling world. It was dark and seemingly empty; yet I couldn't understand why I felt drawn to this spot. Thoughts of all kinds would pop into my head.

---

2   Psalm 134

Teresa of Avila has an interesting image. She likens the mind to a pair of doves. They want to fly everywhere pecking on this and pecking on that. In this prayer in the dark when we are just resting in the presence of God, the mind is empty. That is not its natural state so it will go wandering, looking for something to occupy and fill it up. She says not to worry about it wandering; don't take much notice; just gently bring your mind and heart back to the presence of God. Of course, the mind will wander or even rush off again. Again we gently bring it back.

The *Cloud* advocates the use of what we call a mantra – one or two words or a short phrase. The author says an awful lot of meaning and feeling can be packed into one word: take for example, when someone yells out, 'Fire'. There's a lot of intensity in that. We can use a word like 'love' or just repeat over and over again 'Jesus'. There are the well-known mantras like, 'Maranatha, come Lord Jesus' and 'Jesus, Son of the living God, have mercy on me, a sinner' and variations on that. That mantra was a favourite of Dom Bede Griffiths, the English convert who set up an Ashram in India and integrated some Eastern approaches into his Christian practices.

Yet much of the time, we're in the dark. Ignatius suggests that if we are desolate, we might look first to see if we've failed in some way and are being called to address that by acknowledging our state. In the desolation he is talking about, there's not much inclination to pray. Our hearts are tugged towards lesser things. We'd much prefer to sit idly watching TV – and at the end, feeling disappointed that we'd wasted so much time – or read the newspaper or spent a lot of time playing patience on the computer – I hate the word *Solitaire*, one of those Americanisations of our language – anything but spending time with God.

We may honestly find nothing there we regret, so the empty feeling is the sign not of something we need to address in our lives. It's a sign that God is doing something profound in our lives. (By the way, I'm not castigating taking time off for genuine and necessary relaxation. There are times when sitting over the paper or TV or attending to a hobby or taking time off for a film and so on is what our God is calling us to.) The major difference, I believe, between Ignatian desolation and what I am talking about now is that in the former we're not inclined to prayer. It's not that it's not just satisfying. We've lost a desire for it, an inclination for it. In what I'm talking about – the Dark Night of the Senses – we won't find prayer satisfying, but we want God. That's the sign our state is from God. Lord, this is boring; this is a drag; I'm struggling through; in one sense, Lord, I would prefer to be doing something else but, at heart, I do want you.

We're in the dark and we seem to be getting nowhere in our prayer. And that's precisely the lesson we have to learn. We want to get somewhere, don't we? We want to have something to offer to God, don't we? And when we look at our prayer or even our perfection, we don't have much to offer, do we? Or so we judge ourselves. What do I hope in? My own efforts or in God! That's one of the things God is teaching us through this 'dryness' in prayer. God is using this to purify the virtue of hope. I'd like to have something of my own to hope in and to trust in.

I remember some time ago I heard one of the older retired members of my province say, 'In the past, in our formation we thought humiliation would teach us our nothingness. Now I know that's not the way to go. God will teach us our nothingness'. In the dryness of our prayer, God is drawing, perhaps dragging us reluctantly, down a way that is painful. It can't be otherwise. We want to have something of our own. God is showing us that all is gift. So our prayer is dark and empty and nothing seems to happen for a lot of the time. The *Cloud* urges us to stay in the dark. It's not pleasant and it's not satisfying to our egos; but it's there we learn that all is gift and I have nothing to offer.

One temptation is to try harder. Our experience of prayer in this situation is not 'desolation' in the Ignatian sense where we are besieged by a spirit contrary to God. We want God. God is active here. God is doing things. In John of the Cross' words it's the *Dark Night of the Senses* as distinct from the excruciating experience he calls the *Dark Night of the Spirit*. It serves no purpose trying harder using the old ways, the discursive or reflective thinking, the use of the imagination. Indeed John of the Cross spends a huge amount of Book 3 of the *Living Flame of Love* berating spiritual directors who keep the directees using the old methods of prayer when they should be helping them to understand how God is acting here.

We'd like to use our imagination. We'd like to have a lot of thoughts and reflections that boost our spirit and give us new insight into God. Indeed, we might try to do a lot of imagining and reflecting and thinking. Somehow, we're dissatisfied. It's not working. We just want to be there with God but we don't seem even to be able to do that as our mind and heart wander off on their own journeys.

So what is God doing? First of all, God is asking us to let God be God. God is too grand to be grasped by our thoughts and imaginings. We can't contain God in them. Our ordinary human faculties – our imaging, our discursive reasoning – can't take us to God. God is teaching us not to rely on them; not to put our hope in them and in ourselves. God is teaching us to put our hope in God. God is teaching us to come to the understanding and acceptance of the fact I cannot come to know and be in union with God by my own power or through my own faculties. If you just want to sit with God or to be in God's presence, seemingly doing nothing, that's OK, because we can do nothing ourselves to bring about our union with God. It is God's work. Our hope is to be in that, not in our own efforts.

John advises us to stay lovingly attentive to God or to look lovingly at God. '... A person likes to remain alone in loving awareness of God, without particular considerations, in interior peace and quiet and repose and without the acts and exercises (at least discursive, those in which one progresses from point to point) of the intellect, memory – imagination – and will. Such a one prefers to remain only in the general loving awareness and knowledge we mentioned, without any particular knowledge or understanding.'[3] This is what the *Cloud* is saying, too, when it several times talks of piercing the dark cloud of unknowing with darts of love or of beating upon the dark cloud of unknowing with wings of love.[4] The *Cloud* urges us, as does John, 'let your mind rest in an awareness of him in his naked existence'.[5] In both sources, the love referred to is not necessarily a warmly felt sensible reality. It's that desiring of the will, even though it costs us, to keep focused on God, to keep relating to God. The love may not be a very satisfying or heartfelt thing. Deep in our hearts, though, we know that we want God. Our love is a commitment.

In the darkness and the not knowing we experience, John of the Cross says God is blessing us with 'Dark Knowledge' or 'Mystical Theology'. These seem strange names. How can we have Dark Knowledge? In this long, drawn out stage of our journey to God, God is actually doing marvellous things. According to John, God is pouring into our souls knowledge of God's self, of

---

3   *Ascent* Book 2:14:4
4   *Cloud* Chapter 6 Johnston p. 55 (Doubleday 1973).
5   *Ibid* Chapter 5 p. 54 and Chapter 7 p. 56.

the Mystery of the Trinity and of the Incarnation and of all the mysteries of faith. How can this be? Can I say that I have a great knowledge of these things? Let's ask ourselves: do I think I know a little more about God now than I did twenty or thirty years ago? Do I experience God in a deeper, richer way?

I think if we look at our experiential knowledge and not our academic knowledge, we would all be able to say yes. And if you think you should say no, I'd urge you to be careful. I think if we explored where you are at now and where you were then I think we would find you do have a richer experience of God.

The other thing God is doing here is pouring into our soul – or whatever way you want to describe it – a deeper understanding of ourselves. This can be painful. I seem to be more aware of my limitations now than I was twenty years ago. In the silence of the Camino, I not only experienced God in some sort of deeper way, I certainly had thrust into my consciousness many of my frailties. I don't seem, in one sense, to have improved over all these years.

I realise how limited my commitment was and how much more I am self-seeking. That hurts and some of the old spirituality that emphasised we have to be perfect can reinforce negative attitudes to ourselves and lead us to desolation and disappointment. It can lead us to think we're going the wrong way and tempt us to give up. But there's nothing wrong here. In fact, strangely enough it's a sign I am closer to God.

John has some wonderful images for this. He says that as we approach a light, the closer we get to it the more it lights up our hidden and dark spots and spaces. The closer we come to the holiness of God, the clearer we see our deficiencies and what keeps us from God. He also has the image of light shining through a window. We see more specks when a light shines through a window than when it doesn't. Likewise, we see more specks in ourselves when we come closer to God. We see more dust in the air when the bright sun shines through it than we do when it is overcast.

So while it may be painful and humiliating to realise more and more our limitations, it can be a sign of hope. God is near, yes, and we are nearer, as it were, than we were years ago when we had more confidence in our virtue and more trust in ourselves.

If we do have a way of praying that seems right for us, keep it up, but when we're in the dark in our prayer, just stay there. It's the right place to be. Good things are happening. God is doing good things. It's hard. It may be boring even. We will be distracted. When we notice that, just take our minds back to our mantra, or even to the contemplation of some image or scene in the Gospels without attempting to work out anything.

I think this is what St Teresa is recommending when she says we are human and just as we can return to a mantra without being discursive, we can also just return to an icon or an image to draw our mind back to God. These actions just help us again to return to the loving presence of God, piercing that dark cloud with our desires and our commitment and our love. Our human knowledge faculties cannot contain God. Only love can attain God. I believe that when we love someone, we come to know them better that way than by knowing a lot of facts about them. That's pretty obvious. It's the same in our relationship with God.

Take heart. If, basically, you know you want God and long for God then, despite everything else, God is working good things in your life. You may be tempted to question your desire for God. Do I really want God? Am I not too attracted to many other things? If these are some of your questions, cheer up! Such queries can be a sign God is close and stirring us on.

Chapter 7
The Paralysis Of The Minister

In this chapter, I'd like to spend this time reflecting on our inner life, our inner journey. I'd like this to be a time of becoming even more aware of what we are experiencing, of what is happening in our hearts. As you all well know, God acts constantly in our hearts, consoling us, challenging us, inspiring us, enlivening us and inviting us to continue to grow in union with God and with Christ Jesus. God's Spirit dwells there but we are assailed, too, by what are called– in the jargon of the Heart of Life Spirituality Centre, where I worked for many years–spirits opposed to God. It's a terminology used also in much spiritual writing.

We can have experiences, insights, moods, inclinations, inspirations and so on that can lead us to or away from God, that can make our lives fruitful or render them fruitless, that can foster healthy relationships modelled on the Trinity or can trick us into relationships that end up disastrously for ourselves and for those we meet on life's journey. Obviously, here, I'm talking about what, in the heritage of our Christian Wisdom, is known as discernment.

Much of my ministry is in Spiritual Direction and in the supervision of pastoral workers, including spiritual directors. I have observed often over the years a phenomenon that I now call the Paralysis of the Believer in the Presence of Pain. In Brisbane, quite a number of years ago, there was an exuberant priest, Garry Russell, known Australia wide because he was on the executive of the National Council of Priests. I knew this priest reasonably well when I was stationed in a parish in Brisbane in the 70s. We were thrown together on one occasion when an infant, the only child of some of his parishioners, was drowned in a pool accident. I concelebrated as I had known really well the mother's parents, who had moved to Brisbane from Adelaide, and indeed I knew the sad couple too. When I arrived at the church, Garry turned to me and asked, 'Would you do the homily? This is the fourth one of these I've done in recent weeks'. I could see his distress. One could almost say he was gutted with sorrow and shock and pain.

I'd imagine many people have had similar traumatic experiences. This priest wasn't completely paralysed but he was momentarily inhibited in his ministry by the sorrow and pain of this world. As I'm writing this, I am reminded of a much less demanding experience in my own ministry in Brisbane. In about seven weeks, I'd buried eight wonderful old men to whom I'd been taking communion for months. A number of years later, when I was seeing a therapist as part of my formation as a CPE[1] supervisor, I mentioned this experience, for some reason or other. The therapist's immediate comment was something like, 'And you're still grieving'. He was right. I don't think the failure to grieve had inhibited my ministry to any great degree but I wonder if it did hinder me a little in accompanying others in their sorrow – sorrow that would touch into and rub up against the raw edges of my grief.

Some of us might think we have to be pretty macho about all this and just get on with it. Personally, I don't think that's at all helpful. I think that, ultimately, such an attitude can paralyse us and prevent us from living out our Christian vocation of being the presence of Christ to those who are grieving. And, paradoxically,

---

1   CPE: Clinical Pastoral Education is an education process better to equip people to engage in pastoral ministry. It is open to laity, religious and clergy.

if we can't be present to others' sorrow, we can't be present as fully as we could be to their celebration and their joy. Our hearts have been deadened to some extent.

Have you ever noticed that otherwise kind and supportive people can change the subject when something quite tragic or sad is mentioned? They may even suddenly break off the conversation and make off. They can 'run the proverbial mile'. My experience in supervision and spiritual direction leads me to surmise that they run the 'so-called mile' because personal, painful stuff is touching similar experiences in their life. When that happens, listening to the pain of the other is too painful for us. It touches our pain and, unconsciously, we back away from it because it is so painful to stay there.

Some years ago, some friends of mine were talking of two very fine priests with whom I was acquainted. They said that when one brought up something very painful, they would back off. I surmise they had some very painful wounded spots in their make-up.

I have mentioned the phrase, 'praying as we are'— praying out of what we are experiencing and feeling and thinking. I have talked about a spirituality of the heart: about an entering into our own hearts and admitting what's there and embracing it. It can be, at times, a hard place to go to. It can be like going down into hell. We need support and that's why, at times, spiritual direction or supervision can be so helpful.

There's no shame or cause for embarrassment when we have to sink down both in body and spirit and admit I'm gutted, I'm wrenched, I'm blown away by what I'm facing. There's no reason for shame or embarrassment if I have to admit to myself I'm overwhelmed by the suffering in life. I believe if we can do that but share it with Christ, we will be both empowered to deal in a life giving way with those who suffer and we will grow even more sensitive to the excruciating pain we encounter in our lives. Yet, paradoxically, we won't be diminished or inhibited by this. We'll live out more fully in our lives the Paschal Mystery and we'll walk with people into their time of Resurrection.

As I write this, I am asking myself, 'Why am I not talking, as well, about celebrating the joys we share with others?' As I've said before, I am convinced that if we're sensitive to pain, we'll grow in our sensitivity to the beautiful and delicate things in life. If we shield ourselves from pain, we'll inhibit our ability to delight with others and so be less able to assist them to experience in the depths of their lives the mysterious presence of a God who is beautiful and life-giving. If we shield ourselves from pain, we will miss, too, the presence of the divine support at the heart of our pain.

I'll not easily forget another experience I had while supervising some people in a formation program for Supervisors of Spiritual Directors. I was attending to two sub-groups who were presenting cases for supervision. As I moved back to one of the sub-groups after seeing how the others were going, I saw they had finished the session early. I was surprised and when they declared they had finished, I asked for the verbatim being used as the tool for supervision formation. I alerted them to one spot. The directée had been telling a most painful story. I asked the supervisor in training, who had been the director in this encounter, what he experienced at the moment that I'd pointed out.

The person's body language was revelatory. He just slumped and sank into his chair. He'd been overwhelmed by what he'd heard and avoided exploring it. I asked, 'What do you need right now?' He said, 'I need to experience the merciful love of God'. 'Remind yourself of that,' was my response. As he did so, I noticed that he slowly but strongly began to resume an upright, confident posture.

'What are you feeling, now?' I asked. 'Deep compassion,' he replied. 'There's the movement of the Spirit of God in you. Notice it's taking you into a healthy and creative relationship with the other person. Let your words flow from that point in your heart and trust what comes to you in this movement of God's Spirit within you'. Notice that important point. When the person entered into his own heart and embraced what was there, turned to the loving God, his own spirit was filled with God's compassion. He was being empowered by the spirit to be a true Christ to the other.

A better question from me may have been to ask how the supervisor was experiencing himself at that moment. I regularly do that when I see the pastoral person stumped or powerless to go on. So often the message they are hearing, without quite noticing it, is that they are powerless, are useless, or that they can't do anything here. In one sense, it is true that I don't seem to be able to do much. I can't take away the pain of grief. I can't cure the horrible wasting disease; I can't revive the infant drowned in the pool. I am not, however, useless. I can meet the other with compassion. I can empathise with them. I can listen to their story. I can hold gently and with reverence their account of what they are going through.

We all know that the bland assurance that we'll all rise again in glory may not be the best response. In fact, we know it is banal as a first line of response and can be quite counterproductive. It often won't be heard in the midst of the suffering. To empathise, to be with the person in the pain they are experiencing, to stand in their shoes with understanding, acceptance and compassion will be the first steps we need to take before anyone can hear the Good News revealed to us in the dying and rising of Christ. As we do these things, we are being Christ to them; we are mediating the mystery of God through a redemptive relationship.

I tend, more than most, to reveal spontaneously my reactions. Indeed, an English friend of, I think, the stiff upper lip variety warned me once, as she was about to reveal a couple of distressing items about her immediate family, that she would run from the room if I reacted emotionally. We are all different so I'm not recommending you do what I do. I can remember once when a victim of abuse told me of his gross experience that I reacted with shock and horror. He told me later that it was most helpful for him that a priest had acted that way to his story. What I am getting at is that our best response to the pain and distress we hear can, most often, flow out of our own reaction to what we hear, in the way that suits our own temperament. They are seeing in us the compassion and the presence of Christ. They are seeing in us the human face of God, the heart of God here on earth.

So it is important for us to counter the message that we are useless and powerless in a situation. The fundamental false message, that is often beneath a few layers, is related to our self-esteem. If we listen to it closely, we often notice that it's really saying: I'm useless; I'm worthless. Notice how universal that is. And deep down within so many of us is this fundamental self-doubt and self-condemnation. It moves far beyond that truth that I can't take away the grief, I can't ease the pain either physical or emotional, I can't cure the sick and I can't raise the dead. But I'm not useless or hopeless or indeed totally powerless. I am actually a beloved Child of God. I am worthwhile and I have been and I can be productive, through the grace of God, by virtue of my humanity, my baptism and my confirmation and ordination. I am a sacramental presence to people. I am Christ and I am the church to these people.

When I baptise a baby, I usually like to choose as the Gospel Mark's account of Jesus' baptism.[2] 'You are my beloved son. My favour rests on you.' As we get plagued by afflictive emotions and thoughts that disempower us, we need to come back to this truth. We need to repeat it to ourselves slowly and reflectively. We will, I believe, notice we are empowered by doing this. We are baptised into that mystery of being the children of God.

A number of years ago – 29th June 2011– I went on a pilgrimage to celebrate my Golden Anniversary of ordination. I wanted to walk into St Peter's on that day. I got much more than I bargained for. I went to the Holy Office to get from a lovely Monsignor, Bruno Versese, the *Testimonium* that assures people one has walked the Via Francigena from Canterbury Cathedral to Rome. He asked me if I'd done it for historical, cultural or spiritual reasons. I said spiritual, and told him why. He asked me if I'd like to say Mass there on the day. He promptly organised it. His office is in the Holy Office and I boast that I've been inside the Holy Office and not been burnt at the stake for heresy.

One amusing sidelight for me was when we entered the big sacristy of St Peter's. I was in my pilgrim clothes as, on the pilgrimage, I carried everything on my back and so had only one change of clothes. Around me swirled mitred bishops and monks and clerics in flowing robes of every hue in the rainbow. I mention all this because several years ago I was at a book promotion of Ailsa Piper's *Sinning through Spain*. I was looking for the right word to insert in my question to her and automatically, without thinking of it, I asked, 'Do you think people have more reverence for Pilgrims than they do for tourists and backpackers?'. She said, 'Yes'. I was intrigued by my use of the word, 'reverence.' That is what I experienced, though. There was a change in attitude when people knew what I was.

---

2   Mark 1:1

We need to apply that to ourselves without any vainglory. If we are people who listen carefully and empathise compassionately people will reverence us. This is not necessarily for our own personal gifts but because of our sacramental presence. Through us, they encounter the divine. Through us, they encounter the meaning of life. Through us, they know they encounter the Church.

When I was doing CPE units at Heart of Life, I used to try and educate participants – seminarians, pastoral associates, lay people trying to reflect on their interactions with others–to see that they represented the Church, that people saw in them the sacramental presence of Christ and the Church. I am inviting us to remind ourselves when we feel paralysed by a sense of inadequacy, helplessness and hopelessness to remember St Leo the Great's words to every Christian, 'Acknowledge, O Christian, your dignity and don't turn back to your old ways'. I'm not to let the false message hinder my relationships with others. I need to acknowledge that, by my baptism, I am called in a special way, not through any merits of my own but through the gift of Christ. My presence in a special way incarnates the presence of Christ. If I humbly and simply remind myself of that, I will be in touch with the power of Christ.

As I have said, it won't take away the pain of those to whom I am relating, it won't necessarily heal the dying child. But God will be working there through me both on the level of grace and the level of nature. I mention the level of nature. I am here talking about our common humanity. Through my compassion, through my empathy, through my gentleness and through all sorts of other human qualities, the humanity of Christ will be touching these people. Through the humanity of Christ, the grace of God will be gently flowing into the situation. Trust that humanity as a great gift of God if you ever feel overwhelmed and paralysed by a situation. You are a temple of the Holy Spirit and the Spirit resides in you. The Father and Son have loved you and have come to you and taken up their abode in you.[3]

Pastoral Care is revealing the mystery of God through redemptive relationships.[4] When I've become aware of what I'm feeling and can embrace it, despite the pain, and when I've noticed the false messages I give myself, I can choose freely to ignore or challenge them. I can give myself the true message of who and what I am. Then the movement of the Spirit in my heart will take me into a wholesome human relationship with the person I'm meeting. These relationships are the redemptive ones. As I mentioned above, in my humanity, graced by God's Spirit, the other encounters the face of God.

I was fascinated with an experience that I once had in supervision – and I have permission to use this encounter. The pastoral person was relating to a juvenile delinquent who was about to be released from custody. The latter was totally unrealistic about his future prospects. The chaplain's attitude and, consequently, his ministry were affected by this lack of realism. The chaplain was, himself, not accepting the brutal fact of the situation, that, despite all his efforts, the juvenile would not acknowledge the reality of his situation and would not, could not listen to the chaplain's warnings. The latter rightfully knew that the juvenile would more than likely very soon end up back in detention. That this would occur is not a false message. He was really pushing the young fellow to accept this obvious truth. Of course, the latter was so far into denial that he couldn't: he was going to get a job, he was going to get a wage; he was going to get a car in which he could travel the

---

3   Cf John 14:23

4   I owe this phrase to Rev. Roy Bradley, an Anglican priest who introduced CPE, certainly to Melbourne, if not to Australia.

goodly distance from where he was going to live to where he was going to work. The juvenile was resisting every effort to see things the way the chaplain's realism and experience had taught him to judge things.

What was the chaplain experiencing? It was a mucky situation. The juvenile was in a mess. The chaplain didn't like letting him stay there, naturally, and because he liked him and knew that the young fellow was basically a good lad, he couldn't accept the fact that things weren't going to get any better. As he became more aware of what he was doing in the encounter, he realised that he didn't want to 'sit in the muck', as he described it, the 'muck' of the juvenile's lack of realism that would lead him into further trouble and disappointment. He realised that in the past he had often been able to sit there with others and it was OK to do so. When he embraced the fact that this was going on, he was able to sit there with the young man. 'Sad', was his response when he was asked what he felt now as he accepted the truth.

As the supervision group explored it further, he was able to admit he felt a real compassion for the boy. The compassion drew him into a healthy relationship with the young fellow. Here's the redemptive relationship. It's not the pushing, dominating one of 'you have to see it as I see it.' It's redemptive. I'm sure a compassionate attitude has a far greater effect on the other than the dominating one. The former is Christ like. We might ask, 'Well, what good has it done?' Naturally, we don't know but even though it may be at an unconscious level it can still have some effect. For once, the boy has met some understanding and friendship. He has met respect and acceptance. As I said above, we are the sacramental presences of Christ to the other. Here the chaplain has been the sacramental presence of Christ to the boy. He has been like Christ with the publicans, the prostitutes and the sinners.

He was able to do that because he was helped to bring to consciousness what he was experiencing in the encounter and to choose to take up a different stance. He was able to do that difficult thing, something we can do with reluctance at times: he was able to acknowledge, face and enter into his own sadness and grief at what was happening. At times, it's very hard and painful to do that but doing so freed him up to choose just to be present with his heart and his humanity. I think we all know that the juvenile will see the chaplain in a different light from many others he has had to deal with in detention. There's some life, some redemption in that.

We, too, can adopt this stance, this attitude in our daily contacts with family, friends, work and social contacts. In such situations, we are living our Christ-like vocation. We are being the face of God in our world. We are being the channel of God's grace, mercy and compassion to the world around us.

I have discovered, through supervision and spiritual direction, that there is often an unconscious spiritual and theological false message we give ourselves. When we are paralysed when we face situations like the above; when we face the ache of a marriage break down, the death of a child or of a loving partner; when we face a fatal illness; when we hear of abusive relationships and battered wives and children; when we hear the lament of parents about their children; when we see what goes on in the violent places of the world, there is often something subtle going on in us. Not only are we saying, 'I am hopeless; I am helpless; I am useless', we are unconsciously saying, 'This is hopeless; there's no hope here'. We are without hope. We are looking only at our own powers. We are unconsciously expecting to be the redeemer. And we know, for sure, we're not.

It sometimes stuns directors and pastoral people when they realise that their hearts are weighed down by the heresy, 'There is no redemption'. That is what they are unconsciously believing. It's so very important to notice this. Then our faith and our hope are challenged. Then we need to call upon all our spiritual resources. Then we need to turn to Christ and affirm that we are redeemed; that all is well, even though, at times, that takes a lot of faith, doesn't it? It can hurt so much to be in the dark, can't it?

Here we're dealing with the purification of the virtue of faith. We see things our way. We understand things our way. We're called to let go of that and see things God's way. It's hard in the midst of the tempests to accept, with Julian of Norwich, the words Christ addressed to her in her thirteenth shewing: 'All shall be well, all shall be well and all manner of things shall be well.' It's hard, at times, in the darkness to choose to believe that redemption has been achieved; that no matter how awful things are, God's gracious designs will prevail.

Before I had come across the truth in Walter Kaspar, I was deeply impressed with one of Denis Edwards' books, *How God Acts.*[5] God's nature is to be self-giving. God wants only to pour out on each of us the fullness of God's gifts and being. That's what life and creation are all about. As I've mentioned already, in my days in the seminary, we had those great mediaeval and scholastic tags. The one that comes to mind here is, 'Bonum est diffusivum sui'. Goodness just spreads itself abroad. It's hard to hold onto that when things are at their nadir. Perhaps one of the ways to start is to sit with Jesus as he looks down on Jerusalem and weeps, 'Jerusalem, Jerusalem, if you, too, had only recognised on this day the way to peace!'[6] But we can share our inner turmoil with Christ. We can contemplate him grieving. We can accompany him on his journey into his heart. That journey will sustain ours.

---

5   Denis Edwards was a priest of the Adelaide Archdiocese and a prominent theologian.

6   Luke 19:41-44

What I'm interested in encouraging is a willingness to own what we feel and experience; to acknowledge our emotional reactions and our thought processes no matter how hard it is to stay with them. Then we need to recognise which are in alignment with God's call and which are undercutting God's work in us and in our ministry. This is discernment. If we can do this and choose to follow Christ into the darkness and the light, we'll be better able to live out our vocation as a member of Christ's body and as an agent of the Kingdom of God.

We have, at times, to journey into our own inner hell. I don't want to sound too grim here. Perhaps we can reduce it to purgatory. At least, we have to journey into our underworld, to share the dying of Christ so that we can share his rising. In all the great literature of the world, no one descends into the underworld without a guide. Dante had Virgil when he went into the *Inferno* and the *Purgatorio* before he was led into Paradise. Aeneas, himself, in the *Aeneid* had a guide, too, if I remember rightly, his father Anchises. Orpheus was to accompany Eurydice but he mucked it up. Only Christ went into Hell without a guide.

So if we are to come to know ourselves and what motivates us, what guides us in our relationships and life, what inhibits us and tends to undermine God's work in us then it is mighty helpful to have a guide – be it a spiritual director or a supervisor, or both. When we can journey into our own underworld, we'll be much more able to accompany others on their journey. We'll be much better able to 'sit with them in the muck', as I mentioned above.

Maybe we can spend some time asking God to bring to mind incidents in our own life from which God wants us to learn something. They may be times of sorrow or paralysis. They may be times of joy and celebration in which we realised: 'Hey, the hand of God was there. That's the way to go'. I am sure it's a way to sustain ourselves: to know we are supported and encouraged by someone greater than ourselves, our God and friend Jesus Christ. We'll be able to hope against hope.

I am sure it will sustain and, in fact, buoy up our morale in those times when we find it flagging. The dying is always followed by the rising. That's the rule in creation; that's the rule in history; that's the way with Christ. We share his dying and it hurts; but we share his rising and that gives life.

Chapter 8
The Passion Of Christ

As I mentioned in the introduction, this book began as a series of talks to a group of priests for their annual retreat. This present section was the homily at a Rite of Reconciliation. It was where I briefly treated of Christ's Passion. I have expanded the homily a little here.

The morning I wrote this, I read of the two Christians in Pakistan tortured and burned alive by a mob after allegations of blasphemy. What was behind it? I guess we'll never know. Was it the using of such a law to settle old scores or was it a mad and fanatical expression of religious bigotry or what?

They weren't spared. It's in that light that we look at Paul's words about the Father not sparing even his son. That can sound as if his crucifixion was a punitive act, as if the Father was torturing Christ instead of us. It's not! As we look at the cross and the mangled broken figure on it, we see, not someone, destroyed in a punitive act, but someone seeking to love to the full and to free everyone from oppression and bondage. We see someone who came to free us from all that binds us up and from which we cannot even begin to free ourselves. And in the empire of this world, those who gain from the bondage and oppression of others will not spare those motivated by love to challenge this mind set and to call them to renewed attitudes that allow all to go free.

It was evil people, not God the Father, who did not spare the Son Jesus.

When we read the Gospel accounts, we notice that the Gospel writers did not focus on the excruciating torments. Just imagine what it would be like to be flogged by brutal, sadistic, perhaps, even, psychopathic individuals who relished the tormenting of others. Jesus was flogged with whips to which were attached lumps of metal.

Just imagine the crowning with thorns. I'm sure that wasn't done gently. Then he had to drag the cross all the way to Calvary. So weak was he that the soldiers pressganged Simeon the Cyrene to help him. Next, when stripped, we can imagine the congealed blood ripping away more of the tattered skin. Then came the nailing through the wrists and the heels and after that came the hanging in pain and desolation on the cross.

As we know, the death of a crucified person was brought about by suffocation. The person hanging in such a position could not breathe unless he forced himself up on his nailed heels. That's why the legs of those crucified with Jesus were broken. They could no longer lift themselves up and so suffocated more quickly.

I won't delay on the graphic horror of it all. I write these few lines to remind ourselves of how many of our fellow human beings have suffered torture and excruciating cruelty down the ages. Jesus entered fully into our world. He shared its depths with us. He has a very deep insight into what we go through and into what we inflict on one another. We read in the Epistle to the Hebrews,[1]

> *It was essential that he should in this way be made completely like his brothers (and sisters) so that he could become a compassionate and trustworthy high priest... For the suffering he himself passed through while being put to the test enables him to help others when they are being put to the test.*

1   Hebrews 2:17-18

Later[2] we are told,

he has been put to the test in exactly the same way as ourselves… he offered up prayer and entreaty with loud cries and tears… he learnt obedience through his sufferings… and became for all who obey him the source of eternal salvation.'

When we look at the news items of the horrors so many people today are suffering–the Rohingas in Myanmar, the people of Syria and elsewhere in the Middle East, the refugees who are struggling from their own countries seeking a life free of fear and violence and poverty and hopelessness– we can ask, 'Where is Christ in all this?' His passion tells us that he is right in the midst of it. There is the well-known story of an execution of a young boy in a concentration camp. He was hanged on a gallows. Someone screamed out where is God in all this? Someone replied, 'Hanging there with the boy'.

Think, too, of the humiliation of it all. We hate to be criticised and blamed for what we have done, let alone for what we haven't done. Just imagine the mockery of the two trials Jesus experienced: the first before the Jewish leaders; the second before the Roman Governor, Pilate. Temple guards mocked him by genuflecting before him and asking him to prophesy and say who was striking him. He was robed in a cloak of purple, the robes of a king or imperial figure. The crowds yelled out for his execution.

He has entered into the very depths of human suffering. So, when we suffer, we are called to remember Jesus who will be with us. As I say frequently, such prayer, such memory won't take away our pain; but we will know we are supported and offered the amazing strength to endure.

---

2   Hebrews 4:15; 5:7-9

We see someone who came to free us individually too from all that we are caught up in: our addictions, our bad habits and our frailty. And sometimes to let go of these ways of ours costs too much, doesn't it? And we can be inclined to resist and reject the one who so longs to set us free so that we, too, can share the sort of life he lived, the divine life of the Son of God?

Don't let these frailties of ours make us despondent. Christ has come to seek out the lost. Remember the beautiful words of Paul 'Can anything cut us off from the love of Christ: can hardships or distress or persecution, or lack of food or clothing, or threats or violence?'

Nothing can separate us from that sort of love! Christ will never stop being our friend. Christ will never let us go. Christ will continue to go seeking us in our wildernesses and bringing us home. It doesn't matter how often we stray he will come after us. He is the Hound of Heaven who pursues us relentlessly. We could say he is the irrepressible sheep dog who constantly runs about rounding us up, barking and wagging its tail. It's almost as if the searching for the lost is so much a delight to the sheep dog that it has fun chasing after us and seeking us out.